FALANG
And other Short Stories

Edited by

Mohamed Gibril Sesay
Elizabeth L.A. Kamara
&
Njanguma S. Momodu

Sierra Leonean Writers Series

Falang and other short stories

Copyright © 2023 by
Mohamed Gibril Sesay, Elizabeth L. A. Kamara &
Njanguma S Momodu (editors)

All rights reserved.

No part of this book may be reproduced in any
form by paper, electronic, or other means
without the written permission of both
the author and the publisher

ISBN: 979-83749-74-17-1

Sierra Leonean Writers Series
Freetown; Warima, Sierra Leone
Publisher: Prof. Osman Sankoh (Mallam O.)
www.sl-writers-series.org
publisher@sl-writers-series.org

Dedication

To the memory of
Dr. *Gbanabom Hallowell*
(1965-2022)
Poet, Essayist, Novelist, with a magical voice and creative mind

The Storytellers

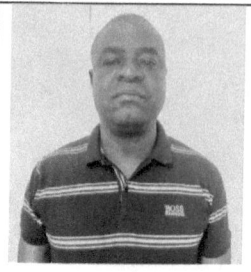

Philip Foday Yamba Thulla

Philip Foday Yamba Thulla is currently the Acting Dean of the School of Basic Education, Njala University. He holds a PhD in Literature (The Temne Folk Literature) and does research in Language Education, English Literature and Cultural Anthropology. Dr. Thulla is also a published writer with SLWS and Ilumina Press.

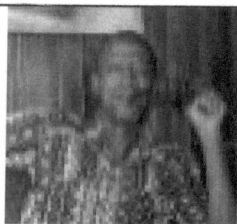

Mohamed Gibril Sesay

Mohamed Gibril Sesay grew up in Crojimmy, Eastern Freetown, and was educated at Fourah Bay College, University of Sierra Leone, where he now teaches Sociology. His most recent non-fiction book published by SLWS is *Civic Society in Africa: Models, History and Explosions of Civic Actions in Sierra Leone*. Mohamed is also a poet and novelist.

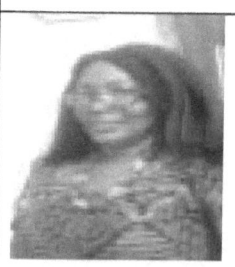

Elizabeth L.A. Kamara

Elizabeth L.A. Kamara grew up in the east end of Freetown and attended the Holy Trinity Primary School and Annie Walsh Memorial School in Freetown. She is an educator, writer and poet. Kamara is the Former Head of English Unit, Department of Language Studies at Fourah Bay College, University of Sierra

Leone and lecturer of Literature in English in the aforementioned department. She has published three collections of poems and some of her poems have been translated into Spanish and Greek. She has contributed to national and international publications including, *African Literature Today*, *Leoneanthology*, *In the Belly of the Lion* and *Revista Prometheo*.

She is among the handful of Sierra Leonean women who have published poetry collections and has consistently supported other writers by writing introductions, forewords and endorsements for them.

Kamara is a member of the African Literature Association, Sierra Leone Writers Guild, Conservation Society of Sierra Leone and Founder of the Poetry Reading Club – Fourah Bay College. Academic Staff Association, University of Sierra Leone recently honoured her with the award of Lecturer of the Year for FBC. She is married with two lovely sons. Her joy is her family.

Mohamed Sheriff

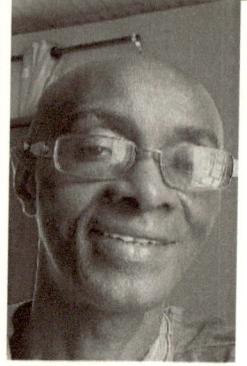

Mohamed Sheriff writes children books, short stories, novellas, drama for radio, TV and the stage. He has won several national and international awards for his writings including three BBC prizes : *Just Me and Mama* in 1999 and *Spots of the Leopard* in 2006[a radio play] and *A Voice in Hell* also in 1999 [a short story] and co-winner of the Economic Community of West African States (ECOWAS) Prize for Excellence in Literature in 1999 for his novella, *Secret Fear* (co-published by Pampana Communications Publishing and Sierra Leonean Writer Series)

Bakar Mansaray

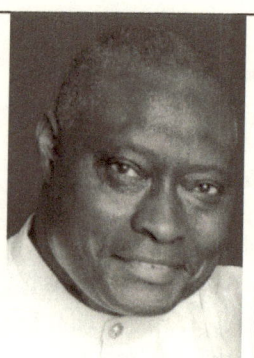

Bakar Mansaray whose works have appeared in the Sierra Leonean Writers Series and several magazines was the recipient of the *Writer-of-the-Year 2017 Afro-Canadian Heroes Award*.

Mansaray holds a Masters degree in Business Administration with research interest in sustainable development. He resides in Ottawa, Canada.

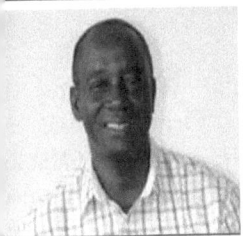

Oumar Farouk Sesay

Oumar Farouk Sesay is a Poet, Playwright, and Novelist. He was a resident playwright for Bai Bureh Theatre in the '80s. Several of his plays were performed in the then City Hall, and he won accolades among his peers. He veered into journalism and wrote for several local and international newspapers. He has been published in many anthologies of Sierra Leonean poets; *Lice in the Lion's Mane, Songs That Pour the Heart, Kalashnikov in the Sun,* and *AFRIKA IM GEDICHT. Salute to the Remains of a Peasant* was published in 2007 in America, followed by five more collections of poems; *The Edge of a Cry, Broken Metaphor, Before the Twisted Rib, 400 Years Of Servitude,* and *THERE WAS AN EDEN* is his latest collection of poems. Some of his poems have been translated into Spanish and German.

His poem, "Song of the Women of my Land," is on the Literature-in English syllabus for the West African Senior School Certificate Examination. He is currently the President of the PEN Sierra Leone Chapter.

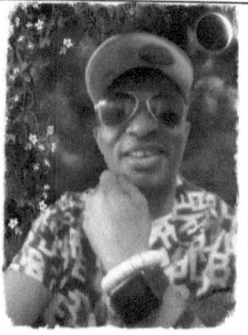

Art Koroma

Art Koroma is a legal adviser and a professional journalist. 'Ordu,' as he is fondly called by all, is the author of Oracle of Success and Holy Axiom. Born and raised in Lokomasama Chiefdom, Port Loko District, Sierra Leone, the author did his primary education at Petifu Lokomasama and his secondary education in Lungi and later, Freetown, the capital city of Sierra Leone. He has a Master of Mass Media Law – at the University of Leeds, United Kingdom, Bachelor of Law (Hons) in Media Law and Criminal Justice – Online University of Pretoria, South Africa, Diploma in General Journalism – London School of Journalism, United Kingdom, Diploma in Novel Writing and Short Story Writing – University of Leeds, United Kingdom.

Introduction

These are stories of magical telling and near magical situations. The stories all have a surreal feel in their telling, overflowing with themes as diverse as love, career aspirations, bravery, and prayers and actions for the end to be beautiful and much more.

Mohamed Sheriff's story "Ndemu, the Crazy Wife of Kuluma" is about the use of stories to sow supernatural anxieties amongst people. It is a story with multifaceted angles and layers of interpretations: superficially, it's a legendary story of a family curse, a ghost story, a love story and a clan's story of cruelty, harshness and just rewards; however, at a deeper level, it can be viewed as a feminist story, which celebrates in our traditional societies, the obscure and the unsung heroines such as the barren, the forthright, the adventurous, the visionary, and the creative and inventive female minds often called the eccentric of women. As a political satire, it's an extended metaphor of myth formation in order to create fear and control to gain undue advantage. On the whole, it's one story that blends the gothic with the romantic while maintaining the tonality of a traditional myth and legend.

Phillip Foday Yamba Thulla's 'Falang' tells of a lover returning from the dead to torment the living. Falang is a dramatic pastoral that contrasts urbanity with rurality. Building on Themne legends, fairytales and set against the backdrop of a village farming life, this light hearted story of adventure swiftly moves from the genre of love and relationship to a gritty and dramatic gothic story centered on the Themne belief in reincarnation – of people who can 'falang'; in this case the apparition of Ruki. But as the poro society and the herbalists brace up to zap the spectre of Ruki, we - as readers- are left wondering, whether the vexed spirit of Ruki –who had caringly loved the disbelieving boy from the city, Pa Foday- will let her troubled soul be wrestled down and be caged.

Oumar Farouk Sesay's "Child Bride" narrates the ordeal of a girl whose dreams of being a judge are threatened by ancient practices. The heroine, Ariatu, an eleven-year-old class six girl had been promised a husband since she was in the cradle. But she was determined to escape the fate chosen for her to one of a life she would choose for herself –being a judge and becoming a person "who stops wrong things from happening to young girls".

It is a narration about the broadening of the perspective of young minds from a village during a career day expedition to the capital city. And more significantly, it is about women empowerment; and about female solidarity and friendship pushing the boundaries of the possible – boundaries that have long been manned by patriarchs wielding machetes of stifling interpretations of norms. But again, even those norms could be progressively re-interpreted and re-enacted. We see this in the final act of the story - the chief refused the traditional bora or handshake during the marriage ceremony for the child-bride, an act that brought about an avalanche of refusal, and set new norms and conditions for the acceptance of the bora, including this: the bride must be over 18.

Elizabeth Kamara's "No Fish on Sundays" explores the dilemma faced by the heroine, Jolit, a woman set in her ways, who is forced to change her attitude to food when she is hospitalized. This story focuses on food and transformation, and opens our eyes to the fact that though most of us eat whatever comes our way on any day of the week, for others, eating food has a cultural or traditional dimension. This piece of work demonstrates that we often cling to the old way of life because we have never been in situations where it is impossible to do the old or customary things.

Bakar Mansaray's 'A Pentacle For Jebbeh' is steeped in narrations about charms, witchcraft, and the fight against evil. It tells the story of a woman, Jebbeh, falsely accused by an evil neighbour, Massa. Despite pressure from the community on Jebbeh to confess to being a witch on account of a pentacle with a dagger through it found on her door stop, Jebbeh refused to do that, her belief in the truth of her being innocent providing resilience against the threats. In the end, through the help of medicine man, the truth is revealed, and the accuser ran into the oblivion of her falsehoods.

Mohamed Gibril Sesay's 'Amina and the Armed Robber's Search for Miss Habiba' tells of the magical reality of love. It tells of how yearning for an ideal lover often limits possibilities of finding happiness with the imperfect persons who are all we have to love. Habib's love for his teacher Habiba could not be realized, and his search for that realization led him into a life of reckless searching that turned him into an armed robber. In the end he finds the ideal lover in the flesh, but then even that lover has her own story of fated love.

Art Koroma's 'The Golden Crown of Ordu' is an account of the magical origins of a man who would become a Paramount Chief. It is a magical story of talking trees and animals. There is the wise cotton tree, the cowardly breadfruit and the kind but gossipy cola nut tree. Ordu, the hero, emerging as a child from a blossoming bud, taught and taken care of by trees and animals, pines for beings like himself. He is shown the way to the dwellings of humans, where his endeavors would make him the inheritor of the golden crown of Gbonkor-Loko.

All the stories go in and out of the beliefs, myths, connections, and experiences that energize the unique entraining of the Sierra

Leonean and general African condition to universal themes of love, friendship, determination, and enchantment with the mysterious.

Mohamed Gibril Sesay
Elizabeth LA Kamara
Njanguma Momodu
Jan 2023

Table of Contents

		Page
	Dedication	i
	The Storytellers	ii
	Introduction	vii

Author	**Title of Story**	
Philip Foday Yamba Thulla	Falang	1
Mohamed Sheriff	Ndemu, the Crazy Wife of Kuluma	16
Mohamed Gibril Sesay	Amina, and the armed robber's search for Miss Habiba	31
Bakar Mansaray	A Pentacle for Jebbeh	45
Elizabeth L.A. Kamara	No Fish on Sundays	57
Oumar Farouk Sesay	Child Bride	
Art Koroma	The Golden Crown of Ordu	89

Falang

Philip Foday Yamba Thulla

I

Pa Foday sat on the edge of the wooden chair fuming. He was completely fagged out after a whole day's journey and he craved rest, but could not for the chair kept wobbling, and he had to work to keep it balanced. He never thought his father would do as he had always said, bringing them here to the village, a place they had left so long ago. Now, they had to deal with the inconvenience of the rainy season in a village! "Such a primitive man," Pa Foday mumbled. This village, Makerie, which his father had so passionately talked of as if there were none comparable to it, was just a thicket of forest surrounding a few thatched huts. His father thought children needed to know their roots, so he had eagerly sought to make this happen. Now his sons feared starvation or brutality from their relatives. Pa Foday's elder brother, Junior, nevertheless, sat comfortably some distance away in a similar bamboo chair. He was probably equally weary, but he hardly showed discomfort even in the face of adversity. He had never objected to their father's frequent proposals of starting a farm in this village or to being sent to test the hard life here. He didn't mind being initiated into the Poro society and many more out of touch groups. That's why Pa Foday was angry with his brother sometimes. Junior had had nothing much to lose back in town. "He is not the kind of guy girls will miss," Pa Foday mumbled, looking crossly at Junior sauntering about, for he was now deeply involved in the game the dirty-looking boys their uncle had introduced to them as cousins were playing a few meters away. The urge to join them pressed, but Pa Foday resisted; he was not ready for any joy just yet. The heat of anger and longing still burned inside him. He was resolute that this time—no matter what attraction presented itself—he would not be lulled by it. Now, Papa had done it; he had succeeded in sending them to this godforsaken place, Pa Foday thought bitterly. It was almost 6 pm, and the birds flocked as they flew to their roosts. The trees swayed in the gentle wind. Late farmers hurried to their huts, their wives trailing behind, carrying full sacks and babies strapped to their backs. A few strong men and their children hurried by with bundles of wood on their heads. Pa Foday observed every movement but he was indifferent. Thinking again of his brother, he suddenly wanted to know what game they had been playing. The game had ended and they all were walking tiredly toward him. He could actually see the stench oozing from their bodies; they looked like coal miners. What fascinated him most was how quickly his brother had entangled himself with these cousins; looking almost like them save for his trousers, which refused to be completely tarred by the dirt. They all moved past, some with clothes offering some covering and others, bare-skinned. As if they had been scared by some strange creature, the boys simultaneously took to their heels and raced toward Pa Foday's. He edged away as they came scrambling, almost knocking him out of the way. Pa Foday struggled to regain his balance, stealing accusing glances at the other boys and muttering something that was indistinct. The boys could see he was not happy with them, so each apologized. "Tank eh," some said almost instantaneously. "Sorli," a few ventured in Krio. Pa Foday did not reply. He just heaved himself in his seat and looked vaguely into the air. But the boys had all come to sit around him, waiting for Junior who now strolled lazily to meet them, unable to keep up. "Pa Foday, we have to find water and wash," he commanded the moment he reached the group. "I am not washing; I am not dirty," Pa Foday said obstinately. "You need to. Look at all that dust," Junior said, gesturing at Pa Foday's body. Used up, he sank lazily onto the trunk by his brother's seat. The other boys just watched the interaction between the two brothers with keen interest. They giggled intermittently, especially when Pa Foday talked or fumbled about. "Eh! Wata, wata," Junior called out to the boys making signs that indicated he wanted to bathe. The boys looked at one another before Raka, the eldest in the group, offered an explanation to the others although he himself was not sure it was what Junior meant. "Mant kambukor Komoryifor yeng." The others got the joke, and they all got up simultaneously as if all they had been waiting for was that statement. Raka yanked Junior over to the side and muttered happily, "Maskorbukor do bath." With the same gush of euphoria, the boys raced across the yards.

II

It took some time for Junior and his new-found friends to get to the stream. The path was rough, and they had to be especially careful not to end up in the forest that housed the Poro Bush. The pathways looked the same, and only a big cotton tree separated the two bushes. "The Poro devil can kill anyone, even society members, who venture into the Poro Bush at this time; regardless of whether societal activities have resumed," Raka whispered in Themne. So, the boys had to move on with a minimum of noise. The stream was a small pool that had served the villagers for about a thousand years or more. It never dried up, even in March. Perhaps, the trees that surrounded it, making it look as if it was fenced, were the reason it had withstood all weathers. The water was used for all purposes. From drinking to bathing, laundering to cooking, but at this time of the year, young men and women used the stream for frolicking. The moment the boys got to the stream, they raced into it and splashed water about, hitting the water violently with their hands. Soon, everyone was drenched and choking. Junior took his time to enter the stream, but he too was soon drenched by the splashing. The water was extraordinarily cold, and the Harmattan breeze bit ferociously. Junior swam on carefully feeling the cold water stinging his skin, but soon he was with the other boys splashing water into the air. They played many games until their eyes were red and watery. Around 6:30 pm, the boys started their journey back home. The big trees made the forest dark and the pathway difficult to track. As they wended their way through the dark forest, Raka explained the mystery of the stream they had just bathed in. It was called "Bath Mishel", which means in Themne "Laughing Stream". According to him, the devil of the stream attracted people with extraordinary eyes who visited the stream and saw him (eye to eye), then laughed until they died. If Raka meant the story to scare Junior, he was disappointed, for Junior wanted everything traditional about his father's village explained to him. Back home, his father had enjoyed the respect of his comrades in the Operational Support Division of the Sierra Leone Police Force because of the potency of his tama (a kind of traditional protection against bullets and metals). So it became routine for Junior to come to the stream this time of the day and be enthralled by Raka's stories about their predecessors. With a satisfied expression, Junior approached his brother, who seemed calmer now. He was sitting by Uncle Midu round a blazing fire with many other young people telling them a story. Junior and the others quickly found spaces in the circle and joined the group. Uncle Midu, sitting on a mat, feet crossed in the way Muslims would sit at prayers, was an expert storyteller. In fact, he was the village griot. That night, he told them stories of the brave deeds of the warriors of Makerie and of their predecessors. He told them stories of the great exploits of Chief Sama. They were breathtaking, and Uncle Midu made the telling particularly dramatic. He used songs, gestures and movements as accompaniments. Pa Foday, named after his grandfather, was glued to the action, his face smiling and almost glowing with excitement. After the stories, Uncle Midu left the gathering to have its own fun. It grew rowdy after he left, as everyone attempted to role-play the warriors in Uncle Midu's stories. Some stronger boys took the opportunity to bully the weaker ones. Then the game was changed to Hide and Seek, and the girls were also able to play. Often, the boys would hide, and the girls seek them out. Pa Foday reverted to his sworn self-detachment and solemn mood, taking a corner away from the maddening crowd, where he sat alone and watched. Then the game became a dramatic dance, and Pa Foday watched from a distance enthralled by the dance patterns and steps, for he too was a dancer... though not a traditional one. The drama was played as follows: girls took one end and the boys, the other end so they stood in two straight lines facing each other in even numbers. Each girl danced or walked gracefully along the rhythm of the song toward the boys.

Owe inbothr-e   De bankoroo- owo   Owe inbothr-e   De bankor   Kom de nanta mu.

She embraced the one she picked as a lover and danced away with him. Suddenly another girl, much older than the other girls, joined the dance. She clapped vigorously to the rhythm of the song in a way that quickly called everyone's attention to her. When her turn came, she danced with great dignity toward the boys who had become suddenly enthusiastic, their expectant faces stretched in broad smiles. Then suddenly, she stopped moving and moved her big buttock scintillatingly around. The clapping from the boys' end intensified, but it was noticeably dying on the girls' end. The older girl whirled round carefully as pageant competitors might do in a beauty contest, then headed in another direction and danced toward Pa Foday. The clapping noticeably slowed at the boys' end and intensified at the girls' end. Pa Foday, now totally engrossed in the drama, sat up; shocked by the sudden change of direction the girl had taken, particularly the turn it took, his way. The girl was black in complexion—jet black—but her skin seemed to shimmer and her body to glitter when the wind drove the fire, making her body seem to effervesce as she moved. Her wrap was neatly swathed around her pair of pointed breasts and brightly coloured beads were wrapped around her neck. Her hair was knotted in such a way that it curled loosely in one big, long, ponytail behind her back. She mesmerized everyone. She danced until she got to Pa Foday who she hauled up and danced with to the arena. Everyone roared. Even the boys who had ceased clapping roared and started clapping again. It was as if they had just seen Ben saving the day and rescuing Barbie from the beast in a popular Barbie fantasy movie. They both whirled around, hand in hand, for not even the most inflexible religious zealot could resist the charm of this African beauty.

III
The village was not in anyway, a sight to be proud of, especially in Pa Foday's critical eyes. Simple thatched huts were dark figures in the night. Each hut, from time to time, glimmered with a dull yellowish lamplight, and the fires, where everyone, including the dogs, warmed themselves, shone faintly in front of each one. During playtime, food was being prepared and soon, everyone was called to dinner. They rushed, briskly washed their hands and hurried to the bowls of food. Pa Foday and his brother joined the other boys and ate from the big bowl. It was like dogs eating from the same plate—there was suppressed grumbling and shoving as each boy raced to take full hands into hungry mouths. Soon, they were through eating or rather the rice was finished, and everywhere the clicking sounds of licking fingers were heard. That was all for the day and everyone rushed again to sit round the fire. This time, they sat in silence and seriously savoured the heat of the fire—the last action taken before retiring to their beds. As time went on, the clusters around the fires began to dissipate and soon everyone disappeared into their tiny huts. Inside Pa Foday's and Junior's lodge were stored all sorts of agricultural implements and locked boxes set against the wall. The bamboo bed was snugly tucked into the far corner of the mud hut; the walls dug out and stained with black from the pan lamp. The floor was scratched, gouged,

and splintered. The bedspread was frayed and worn, and the mattress was as hard as a stone. Pa Foday jumped in first, then Junior, both of them slim and lanky. The smoke from the pan lamp rose in silence not far from the bed. Simultaneously, they dragged the cover sheet up and pulled it over their bodies. Junior began to snore the moment the sheet touched his skin. Pa Foday stayed awake brooding over the fireside incident. He fought to forget, but his mind was full of the anxiety as he compared the tiny physical details of his town lover—the one who had made this holiday so gruelling—to this proposed one. Perhaps the holiday would not be as burdensome as he had imagined. Perhaps this was all just a joke, Pa Foday thought, turning toward the wall and falling asleep.

IV

It was not a joke. Early in the morning, just as he was about to go back to sleep to make up for staying up so late in the night, Pa Foday felt something crawling on his right leg. He dropped his hand heavily on it, but it was not a fly or some creeping thing as he had earlier thought. Fingers were scratching his legs. He held them tightly, eyes still closed, thinking they were those of his brother. It was not unusual for him to play such games. These fingers were soft and slim, however, so he was forced to open his eyes and see who they belonged to. He could not see their owner lying down, so he raised himself sluggishly up and looked down toward the foot of the bed. There she was, the lady of the previous night, standing strangely quiet. She was tall, much taller than she had appeared the previous night to Pa Foday, whose eyes now feasted on every visible part of the lady's body. She still carried on her head the woven basket, covered with a white curtain. From her waist downwards, a wrap covered her, just as it had the previous night, but her upper body was bare. Her arms were slender and there were thin patches of glossy black hair on them. "Morning," she said in broken Krio. "Good morning, and sorry I...I hit you," Pa Foday said apologetically. She smiled, and lowering the basket, muttered, "Food." Then she emptied the basket, placing its contents on a trunk she had dragged in as a makeshift stool. "Oh! Thank you," Pa Foday said, sitting up on the bed. "Excuse me, sorry to ask, but are you related to the Tule here?" She gave a broad smile and her separately filed teeth sparkled. "No. My name is Ruki Kanu," she said briskly. "Okay," Pa Foday said, feeling a little embarrassed by his enquiry. "I should go now," she said childishly, picking up the basket and without waiting for a response, dashing out of the room. Presently, his brother and the other boys rushed in, giggling. "What?" Pa Foday asked, looking at his brother. "No. The food. I think God has saved us this morning," Junior said between laughs. Raka then walked carefully to the foot of the bed and said ruefully in Themne, "She is the envy of the village, Ruki, and she knows it, so she's conceited about it." Soon, one of the boys rushed in hooting and hallooing that they should get ready to go to the farm. Pa Foday and the others hurriedly ate the food and got ready. The distance to the farm was dreadfully long: about eight miles on foot down a lonely path. Pa Foday walked reluctantly onward. It was strangely sunny that day. His feet were wobbling and his head was giddy, but he trod on. Finally, they reached the farm. It was big, about five acres of ground. The families tended the land in common, sharing the burden of taking care of it. Their Uncle had gone ahead to prepare the land for the boys. All they now had to do was plant the rice seedlings. Plots were allotted, and Pa Foday and his brother were given a portion to work on. No play was allowed. When work started in earnest, everyone toiled. Plot after plot was shared till food was brought in by the women. All Pa Foday had feared happened that first day of work. At last, they walked the eight miles back to the village totally fatigued.

V

The evening was cold, but the boys went swimming in the stream. That day, Pa Foday went along, now cheerful. Junior became the guide, leading him and explaining the mystery as they went on. Raka and the other boys seldom clarified or emphasized a point. The water, as always, was ice-cold, and the boys played the same games they had played the previous evening. Junior was now familiar with most of the frolics, so was able to introduce Pa Foday to each one they played. But they were still strange games, and Pa Foday soon became confused. But slowly, he got into them. Not long afterward, they were on their way back home, and Junior told Pa Foday everything Raka had told him. Back home, Ruki had brought in the evening food and left it in the room neatly covered. The boys changed out of their work clothes, ate the food hastily and rushed to join the others round the fire where they could warm up while listening to Uncle Midu who had already settled himself in his usual spot. That night, he told them the story of the girl who followed an unknown beautiful man. Though it was a popular story, Uncle Midu's dramatic telling made it sound new to all. The digressions were particularly interesting and his version had a slight twist. The usual story told of a hero who saved the girl from a man-devil, but Uncle Midu's version was more brutal and tragic. The girl was mercilessly swallowed by a boa. "That's why it is not good to be obstinate," Uncle Midu ended sombrely. Getting up, he folded his mat, tucked it under his arm and walked away. There was a minute or so of silence after the story before Raka suggested a game, but the girls had spontaneously jumped into a singing and dancing session which everyone joined. Presently, Ruki appeared. When the girls saw her, they slowed the dancing and singing down, thinking she would join them, but she did not and she looked sad this night. Instead, she walked to Pa Foday, took his arm and led him away. The night was cold, but the moon was bright. She took him to a quiet place to talk. It was a small square, deathly silent—so silent; they could hear the breeze whistle. Huts were everywhere, but they were all broken. Ruki told Pa Foday it was the "old town." "What do you mean by old town?" Pa Foday asked hastily, for they had been warned by

Raka not to ever go to the old town. He was afraid but hid his fear behind a tight smile, for in the company of Ruki; he had better not take notice of evil lurking in the shadows. "Here is where the old village used to be," she said with a broad smile, holding Pa Foday's hand and dragging him to a nearby rock he had not noticed before. There they sat and she explained all—that she had come to the square solely to seek peace, and that Pa Foday could have rest and all the air he wanted. She was weird when she spoke and often, she touched him but would not let him touch her. Often, she would edge away a bit whenever she found they had gotten too close. So, it weighed on Pa Foday not to try anything foolish. When they got back, they saw the others had gone to bed. After knocking and Junior coming out to let his brother in, Ruki said goodnight and went home alone, not allowing Pa Foday to accompany her. Again, for half of the night, Pa Foday lay wide awake, brooding over their strange tryst coupled to an urge to have Ruki under his power, for his idea of love was, "to get the woman under control." It slipped me tonight he thought bitterly.

VI

In the morning, they walked to the farm and worked. Every day, the work got harder and harder, and the effects began to show in the strangers' faces—they got thinner and thinner and wearier and wearier. Ruki suddenly stopped visiting, sorrows multiplied. So, they lived entirely now on Fofo—day in; day out. This worried all the boys and Pa Foday in particular. "What happened to Ruki?" he asked Raka. "Perhaps she has gone to the next village," he responded. "I will go to her place after work and find out," he continued, reading frustration in the eyes of Pa Foday. When they came back from the farm, Raka passed by Ruki's hut to inquire about her. The others walked home and waited for him to return. He did not take long. "Ruki is seriously sick," he said, letting the sad news out. "She was wrapped from head to toe and lying in her bed," he added sadly. Pa Foday hastily got ready and went to see her. As Raka said, she was totally covered up. She was delirious and was shaking heavily, but she recognized his voice when he spoke. Pulling the sheet from her head, she spoke softly as she told him she could neither eat nor sleep. That she had seen her dead father calling out to her. Every night, Pa Foday visited her and sat by her, watching her grow thinner and thinner. She spoke less every day and her breathing was laboured. She stayed skeleton-thin, could not eat, and could not sleep. One day at the farm, the women brought the news that Ruki had died. It was no surprise to Pa Foday but he was devastated by the news anyway, and his people came round to console him.

VII

"Mo or beraka Pa Foday wufalang-e," Uncle Midu shouted, stopping his work and looking scornfully at the two brothers who were lazily planting seedlings some distance away. The other workers paused over their tasks, looking breathlessly at Uncle Midu who continued to belabour the issue. Finally, one of them enquired. "Wu berawudeke-e?" "Owathfi dis-e," Uncle Midu said, smiling, his gaze still fixed on the two brothers who had been alerted by the shouting. Though completely lost, they knew the matter concerned them for the natives kept smiling, giggling, laughing and some seemed surprised."What?" Junior shouted back, looking at Raka, who was close by, with his twinkling eyes. "Pa Foday's girlfriend," he said uneasily, yet with some amusement."What about her? She's dead," Junior reminded him."Yes, die but falang," Raka said jokingly, and the others laughed at the use of the word "falang" before resuming their work."Falang. What is that?" Pa Foday cut in."Somebody die and wake," Raka said with all seriousness."How is that possible? For somebody to die and wake?" Junior asked sarcastically, imitating the broken Krio of Raka. "Yes, die and wake," Raka confirmed, moving a little closer to the two brothers and whispering in broken Krio, "She go visit you. She visit people and beat them in them sleep." "Visits people? How?" The two brothers asked almost simultaneously. They were now very scared, but Junior was relentless. He thought what they had said was impossible and said so. "Once somebody is dead, that person is dead. Case closed. It is never possible for dead people to wake up again". Pa Foday watched his brother argue, but he had heard of stories of dead people who had been reincarnated. This seemed to be possible only in folktales, but he reserved the right to change his opinion given the strange behaviour displayed by his mistress the other night at the old town."Show me one person who died and came back to life. That people saw," Junior stammered, finding it difficult to put his thought into words."Orwah!" the workers agreed ruefully, but Pa Foday noted that it seemed to be a warning rather than a concession. They worked in silence—he and his brother—but the natives continued to discuss the matter till the end of the day.

VIII
Back in the village, fear shrouded every hut. The firesides were quiet. Unlike normal days when the fires blazed happily and children shouted with joy, now the beautiful blaze of the fires had unwillingly dimmed, and people squeezed next to each other. Uncle Midu got to the fireside, as usual, and set the stage for his stories, telling story after story. His performances were extremely dramatic, as though he were trying to rouse his listeners from their despair and fear. But when he told the story of a man who had died a long time ago and come back to plague people, the people grew more fearful. According to him, nobody was able to stop the ghost of the man who caused terrible havoc until, one day, Pa Yamba, a powerful medicine man of the Poro Society, braved it to the man's grave and dug him out. In the grave, instead of finding a skeleton, he saw a skinny man still there and un-decomposed. Even his shroud was fresh and unsullied. Pa Yamba took the corpse of the man to the village,

cut him into bits and buried each one separately. "This story will come to the same ending," Uncle Midu said, ending his story and then, as usual, folding his mat and walking away. Even though many were frightened while the story was being told, the end eased them a bit, and the games resumed. That night, nothing happened, and nothing happened on the next two nights either. But on the fourth night, the complaints began again and the nights became haunted again—dogs barked and cried; goats bolted en masse as if they were being chased by some wild creature; the breeze grew violent. As early as 5 am, people came out to weep and wail. Those visited by Ruki claimed they saw her sunken eyes as she seemed to make scary faces at them, her laughter dry and cracking. Junior and Pa Foday were undisturbed, and Junior particularly slept soundly, continuing in his denial and remaining confident that people did not come to life after death."If goats run and dogs bark, does that mean a ghost of some sort is passing by?" he asked victims. "It is just a figment of your imagination," he said and laughed mockingly. As days went by, however, the horror intensified and many people refused to sleep in their huts. Those who did slept in groups, for it was said that the ghost of Ruki haunted lone sleepers only. But, as if becoming more ferocious, the ghost started haunting groups and waylaying farmers returning home late. These she beat back to where they came from. Junior and his brother remained free of all this, and every day, Junior fought to get the frightened villagers to be sensible.

IX

The night was foggy—the fog so thick you could hardly see through the windows. The fires could not be kept alight for long, and the huts were closed early. Outside, the trees danced reluctantly to the wind. Over the days, the sound of footsteps had become common, and this night, Junior, for the first time, felt a little frightened as the wind blew doors and windows in and out, causing them to screech. Pa Foday lay uneasily quiet, conscious of every sound and movement. The night was long, and he and his brother kept turning from one side of the bed to the other, bodies tightly covered. The door banged and they shot suddenly from the bed. Looking at each other with accusing eyes, they slowly lay back again. The wind had become increasingly violent, and even objects inside were shaking. Junior's eyes shone as bright as a cat's in the night. Pa Foday lay suspiciously still, hair standing on edge. Without a word, they both understood that the happenings of the night were extraordinary. It dawned on Junior that extraordinary things do happen, though he still doubted that a man could rise from the dead. To him, only the Bible had a record of a man dying and rising again. That message continued to give him confidence, so he called out to Pa Foday, "Pa Foday, are you still awake?" There was no reply, so he stretched out his arm and touched his brother lightly. Pa Foday jumped from the bed suddenly, gasping. Though the weather was cold, he was sweating profusely and shaking all over. His eyes were glassy and full of tears. "You believe these people?" Junior whispered. Pa Foday just sat still, gazing blindly into the night, still gasping loudly. "Nothing will happen," he said, hoping to coax Pa Foday back to sleep. "Go to sleep". He pushed his brother gently back down on the bed, and presently, the lamp blew out. Junior jumped up to relight it, but the door slammed, so he sat back and listened. Then, step …step …the ominous sound of footsteps was heard coming into the room. And soon after that, a bulb dangling above them, overhead, came on, casting a dull, yellowish shadow on the room. A strange creature stepped out from among the boxes. It had the shape of a man, but it was skinny and bony. It was a little taller than Ruki in real life. From the waist upward, it looked like a man, but its legs were mere bones, and it walked on stub-like appendages instead of feet. Around its bony neck hung the string of beads—just as bright as Pa Foday had seen them the other night at the fireside. The creature had a long cane stick, but the boys did not notice it at first because of the dark grey colour of its bony arms. The deathly creature gave a sudden shriek and thrust its bony arm forward, pointing the cane at the boys. Pa Foday half-fainted while Junior fought as the cane came up and down on him. After some minutes, he rolled off the bed, onto the floor, and fainted away. It happened swiftly, and then the creature pulled back the cane and half growled, half cackled, and faded away with the light. Immediately, Pa Foday roused but Junior still grunted and clawed his hands. Pa Foday rushed out, calling their uncle. Everybody was already up; they rushed to him, and he took them inside where Junior was still grunting and pointing at nothing as if demented. Instead of the natives being concerned about his state, they laughed at him. But soon, Uncle Midu came in with a concoction of herbs and smeared it on Junior. Before long, he recovered, but his pride never did. He could not say a word about what had happened. He just looked at the crowd, smiling ambivalently, from time to time. "Don't worry," Uncle Midu consoled, "This is her last visit. Stay indoors. We are taking the Poro devil there now to exhume that witch," he said angrily in Themne and rushed out of the room. It sounded good, but things were going to get much worse. Ruki had planned a much more sinister and spiteful vengeance.

Ndemu, the Crazy Wife of Kuluma

Mohamed Sheriff

Crazy as people thought Ndemu was, no one imagined she would think of doing what she announced one day to her family she would do. A chance happening had lodged the daring plan into her head – *a cocoa pod falling off a lone cocoa tree in her backyard and missing hitting her by an inch while she was half bent splitting firewood with an axe.*

That evening after supper, when she told her extended family, there was first dismissive laughter as they thought she must be joking and then uproar when they realized she was serious. ***They knew that when she set her heart to do anything she would do it.***

Ndemu's husband, Manju, her mother, her mother-in-law and her two cousins all talked their voices hoarse trying to persuade her to give up what they thought was a dangerous, reckless and abominable plan.

"Listen to me, Ndemu," Manju was yelling, "you will do no such thing and that's final. I'm your husband, for once do as I say."

"Manju," Ndemu said calmly, "it's late. I've told you. Stop yelling. Our neighbours will soon start coming to find out what's going on."

"Just tell me you'll give up your crazy plan!" Manju snapped.

"Calm down, Manju. This is so unlike you."

They went on and on with neither prevailing until the other family members retired.

"Don't you want us to improve our lot, Manju?"

"We're doing fine!"

"Why should you be satisfied with less when we can have more?"

"Ndemu, you are no stranger in this town, so I need not tell you the history of old Kuluma."

"You mean the myth."

"Of all the crazy things you've done - this one, the one you're planning – I can't believe it. It's true what the people say," her husband said in exasperation.

"That I'm crazy?"

"Yes!"

Ndemu burst into loud laughter.

She had become a legend in her little town of Kuluma for her daring behaviour that was seen as simply outrageous in a woman by the conservative, patriarchal Kuluman standards. Like when she told the town chief not to interrupt her while she was explaining her side of a case and was made to pay a fine of half a sack of rice. Or when she set fire to a hut which she suspected her husband was using as his secret love nest, while the husband was supposedly in there with his lover, forcing the two people inside to run outside naked for dear life. It turned out that it was another man, a well respected man in the community, with the wife of his best friend.

She was a strikingly handsome woman in her late thirties, tall and sturdily built without losing her feminine grace, which made her irresistible to the men folk of Kuluma who loved full-figured graceful women. Many eyed her longingly. But no one dared approach her with amorous intents. This was not just because she was married or because they knew she loved and was faithful to her seemingly henpecked husband, for many decent Kuluman wives had succumbed to temptations of wily Kuluman men. No one dared simply because she was the crazy Ndemu of Kuluma who no man trifled with. The chiefdom speaker knew only too well how costly it was to make a pass at Ndemu. She knocked off his two front teeth when he pressed his hand on her bottom in a crowded public gathering where people were jostling each other as they moved along. He swore it was an accidental touch.

"Well people get injured in accidents," Ndemu retorted. "Next time, be careful how you move in a crowd so you don't make such offensive accidents."

She walked with the air of someone going to do some urgent

business, which was often the case as she was an industrious woman who used every opportunity and available time to make more money to augment the meagre family income from their farm.

She collected and brought firewood from the surrounding forests. She would then loaded them on her two-wheel push cart which hired hands took to the main highway five miles from Kuluma to sell. She sold various fruits according to the seasons. Around her husband's cocoa farm, she grew vegetables and crops like plantain, cassava and cocoa yam for sale. She needed all the extra money to help her husband support their two old mothers and their three children whom they had sent to attend a new missionary school in Jimbi, a big town fifty miles south of Kuluma.

***

It was in the dead of the night a week later that she put her plan into execution. She slipped out of the house when everyone was in bed, but they heard her because no one was asleep. They were waiting. Deep in the woods she felt exhilarated that she was going on her mission at last. The night was so dark that even with the aid of her tiny torchlight she lost her way twice. Having been rejected by everyone including dishearteningly her husband, she had decided to undertake the venture alone.

When the word got out in Kuluma about what Ndemu was planning to do, there was widespread consternation edging on panic just as it happened when she had told her family. People dreaded the repercussions of her action on the town especially those living in the section bordering the abandoned village of the old Kuluma.

For all her excesses people loved and admired her for many reasons. She was a good wife to her seemingly henpecked husband, who would openly and unashamedly say he was happy to be henpecked if that was what people thought of him.

Ndemu was hard working, forthright, honest and a champion of the disadvantaged. She got into trouble often for speaking her mind against the rich and powerful in defense of the ordinary people. She was also very generous – helping the poor here and there with some cassava, some rice or vegetable, firewood or anything else they may need. But that plan of hers turned even her friends and admirers against her.

The chief summoned her and warned her to desist from undertaking such a venture. **_Pa Kongo who lived at the edge of old Kuluma and whose family was the only one to have lived there for close to a century paid a visit to Ndemu and her husband telling her what he had seen and heard with his own eyes and ears and warned her to back off._** But Ndemu remained undaunted and determined to go ahead.

So she arrived in old Kuluma through the bush path and across a valley and sat under a huge mango tree some fifty yards from a house across what used to be the main street of old Kuluma. She sat on the side of the tree away from the house so she could not be seen from there. She listened keenly for sound of any activity and every now and again she would peep round the tree into the darkness. It was the strange and frightening story behind this house, the mango grove on one side of it and the large cocoa farm at the back that had caused so much uproar when Ndemu announced her decision to embark on her adventure.

***

She had been told the story which was nearly a century old over a hundred times since she was born. The house and three others behind it belonged to the Jinja family who were the wealthiest in the entire Garr region. They owned the only cocoa farm in Kuluma, which was the largest in the surrounding villages and towns. They made their fortune by selling cocoa beans to middle men who came from different parts of Garr and beyond. Almost the entire village of Kuluma worked on their farm, weeding, brushing, harvesting, drying, bagging and storing the cocoa beans for the middlemen to buy. In return for their labour the villagers were paid with measures of cocoa beans, which they also sold to the buyers or at markets in nearby big towns on market days. The mango grove at the side of the house bore large juicy mangoes, which the Jinjas shared with the villagers. The family was well respected and loved by the people because of their kindness and generosity.

And then one year misfortune befell the family.

They were afflicted by a strange illness that wiped out all but one member of the family. First, old man Jinja got ill and died. And then one by one his twelve children and three of his wives died of the same strange illness that caused severe bleeding, diarrhea and vomiting. Mammy Ginn, his first wife who had no children was the only one to survive. Kuluma was stunned and baffled. How could that have happened to such a good family? Was it an ancient curse upon this family? Or did the old man and his ancestors sign a pact with the devil to acquire their riches? In the end they concluded it must have been witchcraft and the culprit, Mammy Ginn, the barren wife. That was when the old woman's real woes began - isolated, shunned and abused by the villagers. Children in particular enjoyed taunting and throwing things at her. Unable to tend to her farm, she watched helplessly as the villagers whom her family had supported over the years takeover the farm and mango grove, stealing and selling her crops at will. The chief and council of elders who believed she was evil turned a blind eye to the pillaging.

One evening the villagers saw her performing a strange ritual. She lit a big fire in front of the main house, collected some cocoa pods and unripe mangoes, and threw them in the fire. Walking around the fire in a red, white and black gown decked with cowrie shells, goat horns and some dried chicken feet, she called on the spirits of darkness to destroy anyone who stole her property just like the fire was destroying the mango and cocoa fruits. It was a frightening spectacle which shook many villagers, some of whom stayed away from her property. But others continued to steal her cocoa crop, laughing at the foolish fears of those who stopped. When the mangoes grew ripe the villagers invaded her compound and in one day not a single mango was left on any tree in the grove. That night a child got ill, showing similar symptoms of the disease that wiped out Mammy Ginn's family. The child died by daybreak and in the following day the entire family got ill and died too. In the space of three days four other families were wiped out by the strange disease.

Kuluma was in a state of panic. Something must be done before the entire village was wiped out. Some people started leaving. They remembered Mammy Ginn's curse. Someone suggested they returned the mangoes. Within an hour Mammy Ginn's compound was littered with what remained of her stolen mangoes. The old woman came out to watch the panic stricken villagers returning her mangoes. In a weird screeching voice she burst into a loud derisive laughter which both frightened and angered the villagers. Someone threw a mango at her, hitting her squarely in the face. She dropped to the ground. Another person pelted her with another mango. And then the Kulumans went into a frenzy stoning her until she lay lifeless. By the time the chief and some elders arrived to stop the lynching it was too late. She died cursing not only her assailants and those who would steal her crops but the entire Kuluman population and their generations yet unborn. She vowed to return to watch over her land and harass them until they all left the village.

A powerful herbalist from a nearby town was invited by the chief to undo the curse of Mammy Ginn. First he performed a ceremony to unravel the mystery of the strange illness that had killed so many people in Kuluma starting with the Jinjas. The findings of the herbalist caused dismay in Kuluma: Mammy Ginn was no witch; she was not responsible for the death of her family. Strange as the deaths might have appeared to the Kulumans, they were not the result of her witchcraft. The Kulumans had taunted, tortured and finally murdered an innocent woman. The herbalist could not undo the curse she had pronounced on them; even if he could he would not do it. For the sake of the innocent ones among them they would be well advised to leave the village and resettle elsewhere. A week later Kuluma was empty. They chose a settlement just six miles away which expanded over the years until it got so close to the old village that no one dared settle beyond that point. No one ventured there for a few years. The mangoes and cocoa ripened by themselves, fell off the trees and rot with bats, monkeys and other animals having regular feasts. Those who dared pass nearby described the smell of rotten fruits as overwhelming, saturating the air around the old village and spreading to the edges of the new Kuluma.

So the old village remained uninhabited until one year when old man Kongo, a prominent elder, was banished with his family from the new settlement. He and his family were found guilty of stealing crops from other people's barns at night to stock their own. Rather than go to another village or town, he chose to return and resettle in the old village even though he was barred from having any dealings with the people of the new settlement. He set up house far away from the haunted farm and on the very edge of the village on the side away from the new Kuluma. He continued to stay even when the eerie sounds started coming from the Mammy Ginn's compound and cocoa farm on specific days of the week and at specific times of the year as if in protest against the family that dared to return to the cursed village. Kongo and his family stayed even when the houses and compound that had been overgrown with weeds and over flowing with rotten mangoes were mysteriously cleaned and the cocoa farm tended to. Even when the mangoes and cocoa were mysteriously harvested and taken to no one knew where, the stubborn old man stayed with his family in the village. The Kulumans at the new settlement had no doubt what was going on. The ghost of Mammy Ginn had returned with the rest of her family to repossess their property. They predicted death and destruction for the stubborn crooked old Kongo and his family if he did not leave the village.

***

That was several decades ago. The older members of that generation of Kulumans had all long since gone to join Mammy Ginn and her family in the other world. The new settlement had grown into a town, but the mysterious harvests and eerie cries from the abandoned village had continued to haunt several generations of Kulumans. And the descendants of the Kongo family stayed on in the old Kuluma . They had become prosperous and the crime of their great ancestors forgiven. They were now accepted by the people of the new Kuluma.

While Ndemu had no reason to doubt most of the dark history of old Kuluma, she had always been skeptical about just one element of it. She felt that the mystery of the harvested farm and eriee cries, if only people had dared to explore it, might have been unraveled to reveal a more earthly and rational explanation. She would argue with her husband many times that if ghosts could do so well, then the living should do better. **So when the cocoa pod from the lone tree in her backyard next to their farm missed hitting her head, she thought of the Mammy Ginn's cocoa farm in old Kuluma; she thought of the wealth that was being harvested there year in year out since the dramatic incidents that took place there close to a century ago; and then the idea struck her.**

It was daring but simple: she would keep vigil outside the house one night to find out what exactly went on. She would hide somewhere and keep watch while the supposed ghosts would be harvesting the crops as it was the harvest season. If they turned out to be real ghosts, she would forget about the farm for good. But if as she suspected some smart people had been fooling the entire Kuluma for generations while enriching themselves then she would go in for her share of the farmland. She had believed her husband would come with her, but he had refused, which both surprised and hurt her deeply. About town too she revealed her plans to some trusted friends and tried to convince them to join her. No one dared. They all feared the ancient curse.

She had dared and was here all by herself. It was a Thursday, and well past midnight - the ghosts should have started their eerie screeching and howling by now. She must have dosed off for suddenly things began to happen and in quick successions. First she was startled as the silence of the night was rent by the howling and screeching so familiar yet so disturbing to people of Kuluma. Next, she felt the presence of something behind her. And then a jute sack was slipped over her head; strong hands grabbed her and lifted her off the ground. Her screams of protest and fear as she was carted away were drowned by the howling and screeching which grew louder and eerier. She felt herself being carried along by strong arms for about a hundred yards through open space and then into a house where she was flung on a bed with stuffed grass mattress. The sack was removed from her head but she was gagged and blind folded.

For four nights and days no one spoke to her except to warn her not to try to escape or scream unless she wanted to be killed. She had no plans to make any attempt to escape in her state of captivity. She knew she was in the haunted house but with the blindfold she could not assess her chances of escape. Even if they didn't kill her, she could get hurt. From the sound of their back and forth movement she knew her captors were many. She reasoned that they had no plans to kill her, well not yet or they would have done so. She could only wait and pray for a safe opportunity to escape before they decide on what to do with her. She reasoned and hoped that they must be in a dilemma. They were crooks but not murderers. They couldn't let her go because she would expose them so they must be debating on what to do with her.

She was accompanied by a woman to and from the bathroom thirty yards from her cell blindfolded and gagged and made to eat blind folded. On the fourth day of her captivity she was allowed to bathe and change her clothes. As she lay bound and gagged on her rough captive bed that night she thought of her family again as she had been doing since she was captured. What would they be thinking about her? She was missing them badly, especially Manju. What would he be doing? How would he be feeling? Would he be missing her? She thought so. She felt deeply disappointed that he didn't follow her. But she must admit that he did all he could to stop her coming. "You can't go alone and I can't go for the children's sake. If something happens to us both who would take care of them?" There was some comfort in that. That was a reasonable argument. It made her feel a little better since that night she left disappointed by his rejection. He would have followed her if it were not for the children and the rest of the family. He had always done what she wanted. With that thought still on her mind she drifted off to sleep and for the first time since her captivity slept through the night without waking up several times. In the morning, Manju was still on her mind.

***

People of Kuluma still wondered why of all the promising and eligible suitors in that town and its surroundings she had accepted the proposal of Manju whom they considered dull and diffident though good looking in a feminine sort of way. What they did not know was that it was she who had proposed to Manju. She found Manju intelligent, sensitive, kind and well-mannered which made him stood apart from most of the young men of Kuluma who were boisterous, arrogant and aggressive. The very type Ndemu detested. Moreover unlike most of them he had had some schooling while he spent some time with an uncle in Bimbi which enhanced his refined disposition. They all grew up in the same neighborhood in Kuluma and used to play together as little kids. He left for some years to live with his uncle in Bimbi. When he returned Ndemu had metamorphosed from a slip of girl into a robust twelve year old who was developing a reputation for fighting and sometimes beating up bullying Kuluman boys of her age and older. She was more than happy to have his mild-mannered gentle friend back. Ndemu loved it when he read stories to her from books he brought from Bimbi. She promised herself that when she had children, she would make sure that they all went to school. Suitors started asking for Ndemu's hand in marriage long before she reached the age of marriage which was pretty early in Kuluma and the entire region. Luckily for Ndemu she was her father's pet child and being unusually liberal for his time and practical, he left it with Ndemu to choose for herself among her numerous suitors. He believed that any man she was forced to marry would have difficulties managing her and the marriage would break up. She turned down so many suitors that folks started wondering whether any man in Kuluma was good enough for her.

"Manju," she said one moon lit night at her backyard after he had read her a story from one of his old battered story books from Bimbi with the aid of an oil lamp. "Turn to me." He turned to face her. "Every young man worth his name in Kuluma and its surroundings have come to my father to ask for my hand in marriage except one . Do you know who?"

Manju shook his head puzzled.

"That man is you, Manju," she said poking his forehead with her index finger.

Manju became as stiff as a statue.

"Don't tell me you're not interested. I see how uneasy you get anytime a new suitor comes around?"

He tried to speak - his lips parted but no words came out.

"Are you afraid I would reject your proposal? Do you really think I have eyes for any other man than you?

Still he said nothing but continued holding her with trembling hands.

"Or am I not beautiful enough for you. Or maybe you don't love me," she continued, suddenly apprehensive, when he still remained silent.

At this he pulled her to him pressing his lips on her forehead. "I love you" was all he managed to say, in a voice barely a whisper. But that sufficed for Ndemu. They were the most beautiful words she had ever heard.

Two days later Manju's uncles accompanied by his rather apprehensive mother paid Ndemu's family a visit. To the utter dismay of all the failed suitors and the surprise of the whole Kuluma, Ndemu accepted their proposal.

Two weeks later they were married. The skeptics predicted the relationship wouldn't last. But their love and marriage flourished proving them wrong.

***

She had fallen asleep again; someone was tapping her. She opened her eyes to see Pa Kongo. She was surprised at first and then she realized she shouldn't be. She recalled his visit and the dire warnings. His was the only family living on the edge of old Kuluma - had been living there for generations.

"You left us with no option but to do this to you, you stubborn woman. I curse they day you were born. Now we don't know what to do about you," Pa Kongo said. "We're not murderers, but......"

"What? Will you untie me first?"

"Untie her," he ordered his boys.

"I need to take a bath, clean my teeth."

"All in good time," Pa Kongo said. "But first, I'm sure you want to hear the story of this haunted farm."

Ndemu smiled.

"You of course know the story about the brutal murder of the old woman and how her family of ghosts haunt this village and come to farm or harvest or weed or brush every Thursday to Sunday according to our farming activities."

"Why Thursday to Sundays?" Ndemu asked.

"First it happened on random nights and gradually settled down to the second half of the week. People quickly recognized those days as the haunted days so no one risked coming around to pry or for whatever reason. You may also know the story of our stay on the edge of old Kuluma".

"Everyone does," Ndemu said.

"Yes when my great great grandfather was banished, he chose to stay here." One night two years after their banishment, great Grandpa Kongo caught two of his sons eating mangoes stolen from the haunted house. They had been stealing mangoes since they arrived and nothing bad had happened to them. The old man thought hard and sent the boys to bed.

"The following night old Kongo and his family went to the mango grove with jute sacks, which they filled with mangoes and carried to their compound. In the morning Kongo sons went away to sell the mangoes in the surrounding villages.

"Next they turned to the cocoa farm itself that had been growing wild for so many years, working only when it was dark, brushing, weeding, removing diseased fruits, cutting down old diseased trees and gradually getting the farm back in shape. Luckily he had a large family. But as time went on the work of tending to the farm became so much that they had to work during the day. The big challenge was how to keep the secret of their new found treasure from others, especially those in the new Kuluma settlement. The old man thought hard and called his entire family to a meeting to explain his plans which he said was to be a family secret that would be passed on from generation to generation to protect their new found wealth. They must continue to make the world believe that the farm was truly haunted and in addition that the Jinjas had returned as ghosts to claim their farm tending to it and taking the harvest to the other world. All members of his family were sworn to secrecy – no one must reveal the secret of the farm. To ensure that no one intruded, at random nights the old man would lead his children to terrorize the village and its surroundings with shrill cries which frightened animal like dogs and monkeys whose cries mingled with theirs to create an eerie blood curdling din. Many leaving adjacent to the abandoned village moved house and abandoned their farms. The old man died but the family secret was kept intact.

"I'm now the eldest member of the Kongo clan and the chief custodian of that secret. So you put us in a dilemma," Pa Kongo said as he finished his family history. "We want to keep our secret but we can't any longer, can we? Because of your meddling. But we're good people. You're lucky. That is if you agree to the deal."

"And what's the deal?" Ndemu asked.

"Here is the deal: we give you a share of the land to manage. You'll find a way to harvest your crops and sell, but you must tell no one. We keep the ghost story alive."

"I think we need to find a way to kill these ghosts and keep as much of the farm for ourselves as we can," Ndemu proposed. "After all the property belongs to nobody."

"But we're now a well respected clan in Kuluma. We don't want them to know we've been deceiving them for so many decades," Pa Kongo said.

Someone coughed from the outside of the house

"Who's that?" Pa Kongo asked.

"Manju!" Ndemu squealed, jumping to her feet. "That's Manjus's cough."

Manju walked in and Ndemu sprang into his arms and wrapped her own arms around his neck, hugging and kissing him. "You came looking for me?" her voice thick with emotion.

"They gave you up," Manju said. "Pa Kongo here discouraged everyone. He said the ghosts have taken you away. But I couldn't sleep; I couldn't bear to lose you. My heartbeat told me you were alive. My heart kept beating towards this very haunted house. Today I felt it the strongest so I came and heard you talking."

Ndemu burst into tears. " I love you so much Manju. Thank you."

"So what do we do now?" Kongo asked.

Ndemu said. "I have an idea to address your dilemma. Tell them you had been preparing a powerful charm and you finally decided to test it when you heard my cries for help this morning. I have a strong spirit so the ghosts had not been able to take me away until this morning. You had a tough battle with them but your charm drove them away finally. You are sure they would not come back so you are going to take a portion of the farm, I would have mine too.

"Hahaha, Kongo said, "clever idea. I keep saying you are the most intelligent woman in Kuluma."

"Intelligent, not crazy?"Ndemu asked.

"Both," Kongo answered and they all laughed.

Amina, and the armed robber's search for Miss Habiba

Mohamed Gibril Sesay

My Dear Beloved,

Hmmmm, our people say it is the little by little pounding of clothes on the rock in the stream that we sum up as laundering. Your letter is like a flower opening up its petals of truth about how some of its other more beautiful petals are closing up to prevent some bug from devouring them again.

Beloved, please don't get into the 'I regret my love' crew. To love is a beautiful thing. While it lasted, *u nor wan yeri wan word*. You said it was so soul solacing for you to love and marry him. You now say you overrated him, and that you regret it. But show me the person who has never placed the person s/he loves in an overrated pedestal, and I'll show you someone who has never been in the happy buffoonery of romantic love. The elders say new love does not know that the waist of the loved one is deformed. In that, it is like what they say of motherly love - no matter how ugly the baboon is, its mother loves it.

So you did not make a mistake, Beloved. You took the path of love, felt happy whilst on the path and only became all-sad when the path ended. Sure, it is human to be sad when a beautiful thing ends. But it looks like in your letter you want to sustain that sad mood. Not only that, you want it to become your main mood, your all-consuming disposition. No, Beloved. They say even the best-tailored trousers for a monkey has a hole for its tail. Even the best of love affairs has its own gaps. Would you ruin yourself because your love has met its gaps?

You gave me Jamila to love. You said let me replace you with her. You said you were giving her to me because it was troubling for you to continue to love me as intensely as you loved the man who eventually married you. You bowed to the ideology that says a woman can't intensely love two or more men. I understand your situation; you left rather than face the contradictions imposed by that ideology.

Okay, you chose the man you married; you bet on him. The choice was difficult, you told me. But you felt relieved. I was sad, yes, because I was not the one you chose; but I was also happy for you.

Love is a bet, a toss up, and you have to toss the coin of soul to enjoy the turning in the air before the coin drops to either heads or tails. If you had said heads for the landing of the coin and it turns out to be heads, great. If not, well you have enjoyed the turning of soul in the air. Don't ruin that memory by focusing on how the coin landed. Yes, the man you married said all those harsh things and left you when he found out about what you and I did before you got married to him. You said if he had loved you he would not have left you in a dry land of no water.

Your arguments in your letter to me are loud and clear. The arguments are great; they are wonderful, full of wisdom. But even the best hat for a goat has holes for its horns; even the best of our talks have their holes: they have their gaps that give others the opportunity to start their own talk. So be it then for what I am writing now to you – it has its holes; so be it then for what you wrote in your letter – it too has its holes. But our people if you really want to enjoy your drink of water, it is better not to think about where the pipes of water pass through before coming to your house. Well, perhaps your husband is the type who thinks too much about the love affairs a woman had before the woman got married to him. Would you blame him for that? Would you say because of that disposition he never loved you? I know, as our elders say, you would not expect fire to come from the stream. But would you blame yourself if it does? Would you blame yourself for how he thinks, how he feels?

Why this sense of so much regret in your missive, Beloved? You tossed your soul like all who have truly loved have done. What is shameful about that? Cheer up, Beloved. Get back to the gambling fields and toss your soul again. You are stronger now for which ever way the coin lands. Perhaps, the coin may even never land - you may just be in the air till thy kingdom come; or well, it may land as you bet, and a greater household, family and future is built.

Don't fret on account of *Congosa, Tiff and Lie* telling your husband about you living with me for a while without consent of your family. It is like I am seeing *Congosa, Tiff and Lie* as they say, 'look at those two, look at them living without consent.' In between these words, *Congosa, Tiff and Lie* pushed forward their closed lips of contempt at us, *shumu*, like the beak of a cock sending water down its throat. Would you become like them? Things happened; we did not plan to live without consent. It just happened that you could not return home during that visit, for it was the night the rebels attacked. *How for do?* Bullets of death flying overhead; bullets of intimacy fired underneath in the dark of the hiding place. Death overhead; joy underneath. Many a child was conceived in the closeness of bodies hiding in each other that January 6.

But, my dear Beloved, let's look at this question: who would sing the songs of the abnormal intimacy of those dreadful times? Those unvoiced songs that want freedom from the prisons of our silence? When will the beaks of the songs break their eggs to push forth birds of lyrics flying up the soul of our skies? Who will sing these songs? Who will write unto them the lyrics of our better hopes? I know the lyrics are there. I felt them stirring in the eggs of the letters you sent to me. And it was as if I heard you say we must sing an intro to the unsung song as we await its singing.

Let's compose the intro then as we wait for, peradventure forever, the songs that, perhaps, cannot be fully created. Beloved, our people say the egg that you have is better than the fowl you do not have. Let's compose the intro. An egg today is better than a fowl tomorrow. It's our call to narrate our stories according to the dispositions of our yearning. Else *Congosa, Tiff and Lie* will do it for us according to their whims, muting us with the shame that they emphasize in the story. Shame mutes. But is shame the only thing in our stories? We yearn happiness; right? Come on, the lord is high; the spirit is nigh. The tree of joy is shaken in a downpour of blessing; its fruits falling all over the place. Let's pick before they rot on the tarmac. Would you let the seeds of the season die in the hot tars of unclaimed destiny?

Hey, Beloved, the fields beckon. You asked for my prayers. Good, we are a spiritual people. But I think it's not cool. This is no time for shouting out 'bout grace in the tiled and untilled halls of preachers donning lazy gowns and blaring suits; blackmailing us that the answering of our prayers needs us to give them decibels of offerings that transform our mouths into loudspeakers for shouting praises. Do we need to raise our hands to the sky like criminals afraid of being shot by gun wielding officers? Do we really need that, to raise our hands up like irredeemable sinners afraid of being shot by gun wielding gods?

Oh, I know you may not see me as unbiased in this; that I rail against the preacher because it was him who advised you not to be yoked with a mad philistine like me. I am used to being called that, a man a little mad, what they call in my area *mallad*. I take that talk as water on the back of a duck. It has no effect on me.

Okay, Beloved, may be, those are some of the holes you may want pick out in my letter. Okay no problem, to each their own; but our people say the joy the toothbrush has to clean the aching tooth is not the joy the aching tooth has.

But come on, my dear Beloved, toss your dice of love again. Don't listen to that preacher. He and his type have been misappropriating the clear message that tells us that even before our creation our prayers had been answered. This is no longer about our mouths monopolizing the shouting of praises in the praying places of spires and minarets. We need to look beyond these divine oligopolies of pews and the rows of safa. So now you see the light beckoning in the fields. Get away from the night. Or as Bob Marley would say, Get up, stand up; don't give up the fight. So now you see the light; it's time to go pick up the grace in the fields; time to go harvest the answers with your hands; time to use your head to get the right pick for eating; the right pick for sowing and the right pick for storing. Our people say you do not cross a river by walking along its banks. So now you see the light, get away from the tiled places, go to the tilling fields. Get up, stand up; don't give up the fight. Let's cross the rivers of doing; let's get to the fields of planting and reaping, that's where the answers have long rained down from the skies – that's where we can stain the answers with our fingerprints.

Beloved, yesterday I went to the barber. But hey, my dear Beloved, it's becoming harder now to have my hair made like I got it from my father. But it's so easy now to do my hair in ways beloved by the *Potho* model. Even my barber, you may know him, we used to call him *Man Na Ose*, the fluffy fellow who breathes like bellows; even he now says, 'just get all the hair off; you look better; look beautiful in that'. My younger sister faced the same choices at the saloon. The ascendant hair stylists praised her new Brazilian hair; the human hair she did not inherit from our mother. Okay, no problem, the more the variety of soups, the merrier the *awujor*. But why should they say our inherited hair growl; that they howl, create fright in the safe spaces of beauty and power and education? Do they really want us to believe that ours is de-human hair, ugly, like the ape's they link us with> Look it up – the ape link - in Hegel, or Marx or Kant, or that angry Caucasian who called our exquisite Michelle ape on heels. This is deep within the dominant narratives. So we remove our hair, or cover it up; it's so easy now in the saloons of Salone.

Beloved, it is raining right now as I write this epistle to you. It's lonely in here. I miss the face-to-face company we used to have. The say heaven is like minds keeping each other company over fine food and great drinks. I have phoned Jamila to come, but the corona curfew makes the call useless. She would not come. It's passed 11 pm. At this hour, the dream is sour; it can't soar. The *okada-man* is in bed; the *kehkeh-man* is sleeping dead. What will I take to go to her, or her to me? No cars are on route; the roads are cemetery-mute. When there is a fight between curfew and rain, disappointments reign; lovers suffer; they can't reach each other. There's love. But how can we move? Too many officers at the checkpoint, ready to put us at gunpoint. How can love ply, when there is no way… in the corona curfew? It's raining dreams and impossibilities. Our people say the tortoise wants to become a boxer, but its hands are short. The curfew is like some shoal shattering pathways of waters; blocking the boats taking our dreams to shores of realization.

But Beloved, I try to make do with memories of our forbidden love - the sins we shared; the scenes we sinned in. I know you say you regret them now; you seek their banishment from your memories. But can you? Our people say you cannot take back water spilled on sand. Today's piety is built from yesterday's sins. Rome's churches from the ruins of pagan temples; the Moghuls made the craven gods and temples of Hindustan into quarries for building mosques; Calvin's acolytes built faith on smashed catholic statuaries. And now discotheque, bars and other pleasures of the new age are established on the ruins of lonely churches in Europe. So that is it then, the successors of Rasulullah, Allah's beloved prophet who guarded women against the ravages of the violent streets of Yathrib now chain them at home from the liberating roads of the new age. Who was it that cut off the sphinx's nose? Whose armies raided Pharaohs' tomb, was it Napoleon's? Which armies decapitated the Buddha statues at Angkor? Who was it that stole the bronze images of Benin? Which missionary tore the attire of *ordeh*, the masked spirit, in the streets of nineteenth century Freetown?

Actions are their intentions, says the preaching sheikh. Our elders say: the fact that food is dropping out of your mouth or off your table does not mean you are feeding a cat. No, that is never the intention.

Beloved, yesterday I had a dream. I saw your husband butchering the entrails of the dark of our past. Our people say if you take your time to kill an ant you may see its entrails. I saw your husband, with bare hands no gloves, slit the coiled guts filled with remnants of the last meal that our slaughtered love ate in the underneath of the forbidden bed. He retrieved those blood-soiled remnants of our final love making on the eve of your wedding. He took them to you.

'What is this?' he asked.

You replied, 'the past is dead, retrieving its corpses is a smelly business.'

I woke up from the dream. I am no seer, but I seek to contemplate the dream's meaning. Our people say **the wind has no wife, but it knows how to unloosen the wrapper of a woman.** I am no seer, but the parable of the wind gives me hope. They say God who gives scabies to a person also gives the person hands to scratch the scabies when they itch. The cow with no tail has God to drive away the flies buzzing it. So be it then with my interpretation of this dream. I am no Joseph, but need I fold hand and feet like the Pharoah's baker who did nothing to contest the dream interpretation that brought about his beheading?

Dreams are irrational, right? They do not follow the realist narrative logic we are used to. So this is the meaning I got from the dream. It seemed as if the sun only hit your husband's back, casting shadows unto his next steps. He brought these shadows unto his wedding embrace of you. Before you met his shadow, your smile was radiant with the sun's rays. His shadows fell on your smile. The smile lost some luster. But the dice of destiny got you to walk into his embrace. You hugged. Your chin was now on his shoulder; your face was towards the glow of the rays. His chin was on your shoulders. But he was facing the shadows cast on the direction he was facing. A tight embrace, but the embracers - the face of one was radiant, that of the other shadowy.

Beloved, the sage says, even with the same embrace, we face different directions.

Contradictions never end; they cohere in us and ours. Our people say the womb that gives birth to a priest is the same that gives birth to a thief. Can we say the anti-rational is the real staple of the world; that the anti-realist may be the real normalcy we seek to strangle with the straight, the linear and the coherent story? Do our people not also say the rain that makes the sugar cane sweet is the same rain that makes the *'gbangba'* herb bitter? But oh, we seek to smash contradictions for the lure and lore of the coherent narrative.

I am reminded of my first crush. It was in primary school, my class four teacher. She was beautiful, Miss Habiba. Like many boys in primary school, my rough games always got me so very dirty. But I got some transformation in class four, at least temporarily. I became very neat, for I thought that would make Miss Habiba want to marry me. And I became so studious; thinking doing well with her assignments and tests was some killer move. Crush turned me into some serious schoolboy; I must have been eight or nine years old. I would learn that her name, like mine, Habib, was derived from the Arabic word for 'Lover.' Later in life, after college, Miss Habiba would take pride in me always being serious with my books, saying she knew I would be a sober bookman. I was like, in my heart saying, this woman, your beauty caused that o – but my intention was not to become a bookman o, it was to get you to marry me.

She's dead now, Miss Habiba. But hey, her looks during my class four years became the looks I look for in love - an unattainable love, she became my known but unknown lover.

I stood atop my innermost desires; winds of joy caressed my thoughts, a picture of Miss Habiba in my heart. But she was unknown in the flesh. My heart was the plinth on which she rose. I lost, though, the capacity to see her whole in the fullness of the flesh. I saw glimpses of her in others. The joy-bringing lips of words, the warm gold of the gloaming dimples, the dance of light and smiles at dawn, I saw glimpses of Miss Habiba in the women I dated before I met you, Oh Beloved. But in my heart I sang of her absent fullness. I sought to dance to the song, but on the dance floor I only felt bits of the soul I craved. The dancers fell short of her fullness. I searched for her fullness, whispering her image wherever I found myself. But do little us own the big images our hopes feed on? The mosquito says, little me own a household of humans I have domesticated; I feed my children with their blood.

Human images look similar. In unfamiliar places you see familiar faces. Is it that our hearts root for the familiar, that we seek companionship in resemblances? My heart saw glimpses of Miss Habiba, rotating on her own axis down the streets of dreams. But it seemed like fleshy imitations of her block the roads to her. Aspects of the women I saw looked like Miss Habiba's, but they also did not look like her. Is that not the case, Beloved? We pour our love on fleshy caricatures of our ideal love. But are we ourselves not caricatures of our ideal selves? Often, others look at us and they only see imperfect fleshy glimpses. *How for do!* We still seek love in the glimpses. But even as we pour love on these imitations, these glimpses, these caricatures, we look beyond, beyond the dance floor, beyond barricades of the fleshy presence. We look over the shoulders of their embrace. We cheat on ourselves, feel pass ourselves, push our fingers pass ourselves for a feel of the untouchable lover.

The cheating forked my thoughts. I could not see Miss Habiba whole. My eyes could not encompass her being; my heart seemed too limited to feel at one go the full circle of the perfection of beauty that my class four teacher had become. My memory sensed her wholeness, but I only saw glimpses of the rotating perfection that faced me. I felt glimpses of her in the embrace of the caricatures. But even those glimpses were becoming dimmer and dimmer. I felt the joy of the glimpses going away. I tried to hug my lovers in the flesh more as I danced to the songs of my memory. But I often crucified them on the altar of this yearning for the wholeness of my class four teacher.

I became bad; I took to drinking, to taking drugs. My life of carefree clubbing became like some dawn-explosion of rays that was so dissimilar to the night taking over my soul. Good people tried to save me; they were like rays racing in, star lights even from far off places thousands of light years away. But my being muzzled all those dazzle. The imams joined the efforts, quoting from books of scroll. Relatives joined the roll, backing their resilience with what our people say, there is no bad bush to throw away a bad child.

But all these hurtled into my ingress of soul. My soul was like some black hole at the center of a galactic bowl. Cosmic filaments of migratory lights, frozen rays of the retro-rational, a bizarro of too many parchments pulled into the introversion of the gravitational heresy of what I had become.

I lost sense of time. You will never know this, but in the alternate universe to which I imploded, events rain down without respect for what comes first or what comes last. Time flows back and forth. That is, it is in the wisdom of that universe that its clouds become darkened with events without people knowing whether the events that will rain down were in the past or are in the present. It all seems so confusion, even in the ways events are narrated. So it is that sometimes the events of a person's death happen before the events of a person's birth; or for a wedding to take place before the bride's own mother is born. But hey, you will see the bride's mother, *Yawo Mami* fully there at the wedding, dancing that her daughter is marrying. And then on the very next day we witness *Yawo Mami* being born some five decades earlier; or for the grandmother of the selfsame *Yawo Mami* to be seen in some other centuries being seized by men of war and pushed down some bad events.

Big words infected my speech; our people say the big word does not know its master is poor. But my big words would not take heed; big words and abnormal thoughts from my too much reading in earlier times; the readings that Miss Habiba praised. Our people say the butterfly that seeks nectar in thorny flowers gets its wings torn. **They also say** blood from a head wound flows over the neck. What is it about these proverbs? Do we get them right in writing them down? Or do we tie them down in writing them down, tethering them to unfamiliar contexts? The sages of Naija say proverbs are the horses of words. Waw, when words are getting slow, they mount proverbs to give them speed; when stories are getting tired, they are fired up with proverbs. May be that's how I use proverbs in this letter, an effort to make baboon beautiful by giving it some make-up, exquisite henna on ugly fingers. Or are proverbs refrains of deep re-interpretations of our narratives? Or buzzing mosquitoes tormenting our rationalist dreams? Are they elevations of the truth of contradictions? Or are they gestures towards the quantum nature of fundamental reality? We are, and the same time, we are not? That's like God playing dice, says Einstein the watchmaker. Or are proverbs attempts at cryptic reconnections of seemingly unconnected but fundamentally connected facts? Okay, what does the proverb about blood from a head wound seek to draw attention to? That my being was in some violent act affecting my relations?

Okay, I get it. My being was violence of the sub-atomic, implosions of nuclei of too many books of fusing perspectives. Or is it fission? My being's surface was some wailing Sagittarius of massive blue suns sucked into labyrinths of an alternative universe – Or multiverses, or … into the core's invisibility of introversion.

The elders simplify and specify the head wound proverb thus: a mad relative dancing naked in the village square is a shame not to himself, but to his family. The efforts to save me from my narrative mishmash got to my family getting Amina, a daughter of a friend of my father, to marry me. Oh Amina, wonderful Amina, beautiful, brilliant, black - she became the safety net I nailed around the tower I was building to get to the sky of my mad dreams; a moral safety net for falling into.

In my invisibility of introversion, I was building a tower, some Babel of power from which to launch my spaceship. I cared little. The safety net insured my bravery. All my mistakes fell on Amina - oh Amina, wonderful Amina, beautiful, brilliant, black. I myself fell on her, with my tools and blocks and concrete. I picked myself up from her and continued my assault on the sky.

The preaching sheikh encouraged her with these words: 'you are Amina, your name means safety, be that being of safety for your husband, be his rest from his restlessness. Remember this: wives seek heaven at the feet of their husbands.'

Amina stayed for a while in that crazy mental space of mine; nailed midway between heaven and mud; between the astronomy of my hopes and the geology of my fall.

One day she told me she wanted to free herself from the nails of my schizophrenic ambition, from the immorality of my fall. She said, 'your pain I note, but your pain I cannot tote; your pain I feel, but your pain I cannot fell.'

I asked, 'why the so many 'buts' in your speech?'

She replied, 'your speech is infecting me, you have 'buts' in almost everything you say. Even when you text me, they are full of 'buts.' You think too way self-contradictorily, butting your own thoughts with 'buts' and 'buts' and 'buts,' gorging your sentences. You give your speech and texts and stories too many mental wounds, too many unhealed sores, and sometimes their smells are not good at all. We really cannot stay together. I must leave you.'

Oh Amina, wonderful Amina, beautiful, brilliant, black, she was sick of inhaling my smelly feet. She was no crooked rib; she was not the bent side of me that got gotten out by God. She was not the bony sickle of moral failure who got nailed with the rogue proverb: woman was created from a bent bone; he who tries to straighten her breaks her. Amina was tired of me falling unto her; she wanted to float away; she would no more be no one's safety net.

Our people say he who beats a drum for a madman to dance is also mad. I hope you see the inside of these proverbs: that piece of meat you don't want to eat, don't use your teeth to cut and share it; if you don't want the tail of a monkey to touch you, don't go to a party for monkeys. Oh Amina, wonderful Amina, beautiful, brilliant, black, she was tired of the monkey's tail touching her; she would no longer cut with her teeth meat she could not eat. Why should she continue to beat the drum for a mad man like me to dance? Oh Amina, wonderful Amina, beautiful, brilliant, black.

My descent into drugs accelerated. I lost my job, but I did not lose my drug habit. I started begging; it was not enough to finance my addiction. I started stealing, little items here and there. Imagine that, a university graduate, honors degree first class, masters degree with distinction. But again they say academic qualifications are not moral qualifications. I continued stealing, small-small items - spoons here, knife there, wet knickers and sneakers left out to dry over there.

But our people say little drops of piss eventually make the trousers smelly. I joined night robbers. I went to your house, Beloved, to steal on a night that was still. I cut the window grilles with a giant scissor. Fetus bent I entered head first, like human birth unto the world. And then I saw you. I froze. How could it be that my ideal of love and beauty was there in the flesh? Just at the edge of losing all hopes I saw you. You were smiling in your sleep; some sweet thing must have been going on in your dream; a thing may be of angels. The smile moved inside me - a vision of beauty; a feel of joy, a taste of sweetest hope. You looked like Miss Habiba of my class four encounter rebooting for the new times.

And then you momentarily woke up, looked at my face and dreamily said, 'oh you are the one, you are the lover I have been dreaming of, but why did you come to me now in the shape of an armed robber?'

I have always wondered whether you were actually conscious when you said those words, for you fell into sleep again right after asking the questions, like you felt so safe, secured, trusting that though armed, my harming you is an existential impossibility. I stood there, watching you sleep, my vision draining uncontrollably into your being. And then I heard a voice; a voice in the shape of my voice but which looked like it was coming from you:

'Love that can't be fully seen
Seems like incomplete love
But are we complete?
From birth our bodies
Never stop becoming something else
From birth our desires
Keep changing with our bodies
We search for keys we already hold in our hands.
We seek more than the bits we have.

That's our condition.
As love rotates on its axis
To reveal more of herself
She never reveals herself whole
Parts of her still face towards
The dark spaces of our ignorance
Our souls spin for a fuller experiencing
Our hearts ache for a fuller embrace
We leave this feeling for that feeling
We leave this glimpse for that glimpse
We are committed to the unattainable fullness
But not committed to its glimpses in the flesh'

The yearning never ends

That's our destiny
A destiny of glimpses
A destiny of intros
To the songs of love
Embrace then your intro
To the unattainable fullness of the lover
The lover who can't be known
In all her glory, all her beauty, the unknown lover
You may sing the intros sad,
You may sing them happy
The choice is in your soul
But as you sing
Never forget to punctuate your intro
With stanzas to the known love
For even as we cheat on ourselves
For the unattainable lover
Remember this:
'Ourselves in the flesh are what we truly have'

Love always,
Habib

A Pentacle for Jebbeh

Bakar Mansaray

The clay pentacle and the black-handled double-edged dagger showed up on Jebbeh's doorstep that morning. Massa, the woman with the jewelled eyes, showed up that evening. The two appearances jolted her all the way through. Jebbeh, a petty trader, found the two items lying side-by-side as she opened the door to walk to the foothills. Her darker skin portrayed angelic beauty, even at age forty, and her full set of delicate lips matched her natural curly, jet-black hair that gave her an air of superiority. Her full-figure, partially hidden by a black flowing gown, hardly reflected her strength. Frightened and then slightly unconcerned, she walked passed the two items. Not until she returned at sunset, when she saw the tip of the dagger stuck into the center of the five-pointed star pentacle, did she become concerned. She knew a pentacle and a dagger to be two of the most recognized symbols of witches and witchcraft. Jebbeh froze at the thought. She stood still, staring at the mysterious act of violence, and tried to contain the sudden strong feeling of fear that gripped her body.

Then she remembered Massa, her next-door neighbour, whom she last saw three days ago. The image of her roughly cleaved features and the glistening jewelled extents of her outlandishly impelling eyes recurred with exploding force in her mind. Her stare never leaving the dagger in the pentacle, Jebbeh reached out a trembling hand, grasped the door handle, and quickly entered the house. The house itself was simply built with sticks, mud, and thatched roof. It stood apart from two other similarly-built houses. She tried to imagine who would have played such a spellbound trick on her. There was the quiet little man, her landlord. Then there was Massa. But she couldn't see the little man doing something like this. And why would Massa do such a thing either?

Anxiously, Jebbeh went to stand in front of the window that faced the mountains.

This was a specifically isolated and barren expanse of Sierra Leone's southeastern region. It is called Potoru, a small town that became lively only during harvest time - the time for the Ndogboyosoi bush devil dance, when people would be flocking in from neighbouring towns. But now it was early rainy season and the place was as quiet as a graveyard. Nobody whom she'd came across appeared to be the kind of person to pull this feat with the pentacle. Once more Jebbeh thought of Massa, the woman with the jewelled eyes.

Massa's roughly cleaved features and her glistening jewelled eyes reminded Jebbeh of the once-notorious Freetown witch, Adama. Massa was a tall, lanky, dark-skinned, girlish-looking woman within her mid-forties. Normally, she didn't just wear her clothes — she hid inside them. She never wore any footwear. She carried her black hair in dreadlocks. Her head always darted about like a radar blip on her neck. Massa liked pacing around the compound in a perpetual motion of twitching, fidgeting, and twiddling. When a conversation with someone was over, she would dash back into her bedroom like a frightened bunny, probably wishing that she could lock herself in there forever.

It'd been extremely difficult for Jebbeh to keep her mind at ease. These two strange objects were definitely not lying side-by-side on her doorstep when she initially came to the house. But what was more extraordinary about them was the fact the tip of the dagger was now stuck into the center of the pentacle. The more she thought about it, the more she was convinced that this must have been a deliberate act perpetrated by someone with evil intent.

Outside, the storm clouds had covered the evening sky. Thunder clapped and she heard the sound of whistling wind in the trees and of falling rain. Jebbeh lit the hurricane lamp, fueled by kerosene, to starve off the darkness in the house. A sense of tightness and hunger took control of her. She was just about to eat some food when she heard a faint knock on the door. She leapt with a start from her stool as her heart fluttered in her chest. She regarded the door for a while as though she was in two minds. Gingerly, she walked towards the door fighting the fear that washed over her in waves. Her fear became intolerable and in a tremulous voice she asked:

"Who is it?" There was no answer. Maybe whoever it was couldn't hear her over the howl of the storm. Taking a deep breath, she asked once more with uneasiness:

"Who's there?"

"It's me, Massa."

Without opening the door, Jebbeh sigh with relief before inquiring:

"What do you want?"

"Can I have a word with you?" she inquired in a lackadaisical drawl.

"A word with me?" Jebbeh mumbled, as if she'd never heard such a phrase.

The smoothness of Massa's voice brought back memories of the last time she'd seen her. It also brought an ineffable alertness she'd not been able to comprehend. She unlocked the door and allowed her inside. Jebbeh recoiled as Massa stepped into the room, her eyes moving over her drenched figure. A stench of stale sweat walked into the room with her. Jebbeh thought Massa portrayed an air of arrogance and recklessness.

As Jebbeh closed the door, the wind howled frighteningly, thereby finding herself in the unbelievable situation that had led to her doubts about Massa. She gave her a long, penetrating look, clearly trying to decide if she can trust her or not.

"What's it all about?" Jebbeh asked, without offering her a seat.

"I saw the clay pentacle and the black-handled double-edged dagger on your doorstep," she said, inspecting her knuckles.

"And so?" Jebbeh said hastily.

"I'm worried that something might go wrong with you," she said, tapping her wet red blouse and black wrapper. Slowly, her jewelled eyes assessed Jebbeh's features in the lamplight. "Folks are known to be plying witchcraft in this town."

"I don't know," Jebbeh pointed out thoughtfully, "but witchcraft doesn't appeal to me."

"It has its moments," Massa agreed coolly. "But the memes of this town of Potoru dictate our beliefs and our actions."

Jebbeh hesitated. "What makes you say that?"

"Don't see yourself as standing outside the realm of witchcraft, as we all have them in us one way or another," Massa pointed out.

Jebbeh slid her a sharp glance, wondering at the unquestionable nature of her words. "You're just full of surprises. I wouldn't have thought it would appeal to you," said Jebbeh.

"Did I say it appeal to me?" Massa retorted, wishing she wouldn't continue the subject of witchcraft.

But Jebbeh found the conversation interesting, especially when she thought about the pentacle and the dagger on her doorstep. She shook her head. "How can one practise witchcraft?"

"Umm." Cautiously Massa kept her response ambiguous. "Some people think beliefs in witchcraft translate the knacks of one's soul."

"I think most acts of witchcraft are steeped in ritual." Her eyes never left Massa's face. "They're parts of local religions packed with beliefs in witchcraft, magic, and the like."

"Something is afoot, with this pentacle and dagger on your doorstep."

"Don't worry. I'm fine," Jebbeh responded abruptly and showed her out.

Jebbeh's neighbour, Blamo, an intelligent secondary school teenage boy mysteriously took ill that same evening when a magnificent owl sat on a perch in their compound. By day-break he passed away. The neighbourhood, led by Massa, levied allegations of witchcraft against Jebbeh. They held her responsible for his death, claiming that they found a clay pentacle and a black-handled double-edged dagger on her doorstep. Blamo was born with fibular hemimelia on his left leg. At one year old, the leg was amputated halfway between his knee and ankle. He'd always been known for determination, eloquence, and intelligence. Few years earlier, he was awarded a scholarship to continue his studies.

On hearing the death of Blamo, the elders summoned Jebbeh to court in view of bringing up the allegations. Three days later, there was no response from her. They sent a court messenger, asking her to make herself available at the town's court, yet she didn't budge. One week later, the chief clerk wrote her himself, proposing a visit. Instead, he received her message, saying that she'd become a recluse. Then a group of neighbours decided to pay her a visit in order to discuss the matter. On that day, storm clouds had been rolling in from the mountains, covering the afternoon sky. They looked at each other as the wind began to hurl drizzling rain on them, knowing fully well that the storm would soon begin to rage. When they knocked on the door of the house through which no caller had entered since Jebbeh became a recluse, she leapt with a start from her bed. She unlocked the door and allowed them inside a darkish, dusty and foul-smelling parlour that sent their noses on a twitching jive.

Massa was among them. The spokesman for the neighbours offered a timid handshake to Jebbeh, but she must have thought it was an invitation to a wrestling match. The room had just basic furniture. As soon as she opened the curtain of a window, the neighbours then saw the dusty state of the furniture. They were also taken aback to see a picture of Nebuchadnezzar who was once the king of Babylon in biblical times. In the picture, he'd long beard, wicked-looking eyes, and crouched on all fours like a wolf. He lost his sanity as a punishment for his pride and vanity.

Jebbeh stood up in a very straight and stiff manner. A black lace veil framed her face and her hair was going gray; faster than a kiss. Since she became a recluse, she always wore a black flowing gown. Once a plump, vibrant and hopeful young woman, heartbrokenness now made her look wrinkled, thin, and old. Nevertheless, she carried herself with an air of authority, exhibiting an aura of superiority that always made people feel restless. For a moment, Massa felt those eyes on her like deep lakes about to drown her.

Jebbeh didn't utter a word as the spokesman referred to the allegations. When she finally spoke, her voice was hoarse and brisk.

"I've nothing to do with witchcraft."

"And didn't you receive a summon letter from the court clerk?" he said contemptuously.

"I did and I responded accordingly," she said, flashing an irritated glare in return.

"But as a good citizen we expected better from you," the spokesman said, continuing to show his displeasure.

"Do you want to tell me how to behave?" she said with the kind of distaste reserved for cockroaches.

"Jebbeh, this will not help you," the spokesman replied threateningly.

"It's none of your business," she said harshly, then asked them to leave.

The following day, there was news that a little girl had gone missing from her family home. Again, the neighbourhood, led by Massa, became suspicious of Jebbeh. They argued that as long as the clay pentacle and the black-handled double-edged dagger was still on her doorstep, then she must be aware of the little girl's disappearance. Frustrated and heartbroken, Jebbeh longed for her life to take a better turn. She'd no reason to think that such a thing would ever happen soon; yet, she hoped, she prayed, she wished. She thought her life might find a spark in the form of love, maybe through a husband, to set the tinder of her dreams ablaze. That much needed love that would blossom like her favourite flower; the feminine tropical vanilla orchid that opened for one day in a year. She understood what it was to want a husband. She also understood how fast perfunctory craving could be illusive. Seduction was an irresistible, if usually brief passion. That was a spell she could cast. But when seduction became entangled with other sentiments like her current heighten sense of fright, it came close to develop into something considerably adept and extremely more troubling.

As the neighbours continued to pester Jebbeh, without neither investigating the allegations nor coming up with evidence, she became increasingly reclusive. Nobody could exonerate her. She sorrowed much. Her eyes were forever big with incomplete crying like a baby snatched from its enchanted cosmos. She was unwilling to come to terms with life. To live was like having an irrepressible sense of ostracism; her feet fluttering in delusions of flight to the unknown. Her nocturnal dreams, often kindled by a spectral glow, were full of long, painful cries of dread; groans of agony. At times, she was such a dervish of fury that she couldn't understood her own behaviour. She remained inconsolable for days on end. She refused to see a couple of her acquaintances who called on her. Then gossips about Jebbeh being a witch spread like wild fire on the savannah grassland of Timbuktu.

Every now and then as time flew by without stopping, her thoughts kept rebounding between the clay pentacle and the black-handled double-edged dagger on her doorstep, and the image of Massa. There was no sympathy between Jebbeh and her neighbours. They continued to find ways to bring her to book for allegedly skirting the law. Others considered the maltreatment of her as not only uncalled for, but as harassment.

Potoru was now a town of astonishments. A day without spectacle was cause for concern. Few days later, in the dusky haze of evening, Kaikai Lango, the town's herbalist paid Jebbeh a visit with the intention of casting away evil spells from her, and of finding the little girl that had gone missing. In his late-fifties, Kaikai Lango was a tall and majestic figure depicting spiritual authority. His thin eyebrows and narrow nose gave him a handsome look. He was dark in complexion, and known to be compassionate and jovial. When he walked, his heels barely touched the ground. He walked as if he was ready to fly. Kaikai Lango wasn't an ordinary herbalist. Although he looked simple, many considered him a messiah who performed wonders for the sick and suffering. He also exorcised witches and wizards. Praises for his miracles could be heard on the lips of the young and old. People from all over the country and beyond came to visit Kaikai Lango. For many, he was as good a man as gold.

Before he was let into the house, Jebbeh was standing in front of her window observing the storm clouds rolling in from the mountains. As Jebbeh and Kaikai Lango looked at each other, they knew time was of essence because of the impending storm. The wind had started to hurl rain against the wooden door and windows of the house.

Jebbeh shifted uncomfortably where she stood. "What makes you think that you can help me?"

"Well, let's prove that these allegations of witchcraft are false," he said sardonically.

For a while she was silent. "What do you mean?"

Without hesitation, he asked with a sarcastic grimace, "Are you practicing witchcraft or not?"

She looked like she was about to burst into flames. As if she wasn't expecting that question from him, she quickly changed her countenance to that of being calm. Then she gave a mock shudder.

"These are false allegations."

Kaikai Lango looked at her and sighed. "Aren't you worried about what people say?"

"Yes, I'm worried. But what can I do?"

He shook his head with a smile of delight. "I'll see what I can do."

At that moment, something exerted her about the way Kaikai Lango emphasized his statement. She gave him a brief doubtful look. "They're just trying to destroy my life."

He shook his head solemnly in the lamplight. "It's a treacherous world."

"Then let them know that I don't practice witchcraft," she said emphatically.

He took a deep breath, and felt pity for her. "Yes, I guess so." Jebbeh thought that it was rather strange for him to have that unexpectedly affectionate awareness of a woman whom they'd doubts about. She sensed the excitement that appeared to have engulfed her. It was a climax of the burgeoning anxiety she'd been witnessing all day.

Quietly he asked her to bring the lighted lamp and follow him to her doorstep. The rain had ceased but a flash of lighting was followed by thunder and the nocturnal cry of an owl. The flash of lighting shone on the double-edged dagger, illuminating it powerfully. Then one of the storm clouds rolling in from the mountains blanked out the abrupt ray of light. The double-edged dagger kept on glowing dimly as Kaikai Lango asked her to keep following him to the far end of the compound.

Kaikai Lango stared at Jebbeh, tempestuously conscious of the pristine lamplight shining unsteadily on her unkempt hair. It lit up her hairpins, making him think of moonshine on a dark lake. Her body, once strengthened by her work as a petty trader, now looked weak. But it wasn't just her physical strength. The stamina went all the way through her. It was a part of her sentimental and psychological attribute as well as the tangible side of her nature. In brief, he wondered why Jebbeh who lived by trading should have developed such a complete, almost cavalier stamina. The black flowing gown in which she was dressed tonight gave no clue of her role in the community, but the clothes did stress the basic impact she made on him.

He could remember very clearly the other woman's last words to him some time ago. They'd flashed on and off his mind along with her image since that day. I want your assurance that you'll never disclose to anyone the story of the little child that you found in my farm hut. And she'd made a promise to him not to ever perform such an act again. He'd understood the crushing force of her gaze at that time. Understood that she meant every word. But it'd never occurred to him then that he might actually tell such a story again. As a matter of fact, a part of his conscience had cautioned that it would be very embarrassing to tell the story. But that cautiousness had caused him, though reluctantly, to seek the truth tonight.

He remembered all too clearly that late night when he was performing a ritual near the other woman's farm hut and seen a glow underneath the door of the hut. So, the fact that it was that late at night for a glow to be seen in the hut had gently interested Kaikai Lango. Other things had interested him about that hut for some days following that ominous night. He'd seen the other woman and a small, lean-looking child entering the hut. The little girl had been wearing only a white loincloth. But after they'd vanished inside the hut they'd not reappeared again. It made little sense to stay locked inside a hut for hours. Then, he'd decided to knock on the door of the hut. The other woman made it clear to him that he wasn't welcomed and politely turned him away. It was as he was going back home that he'd happened to turn around and seen the face of the little girl, probably about six years old, staring at him from the hut's wooden window.

In that instant, he knew he'd never seen such a strange look on the face of a child. It'd shocked him. As he'd stood there gazing at the girl, the other woman had precipitously snatched her away from the window, apparently. Naturally frightened but uncertain as to what might be taking place, he decided to keep a watch on the hut. Something wasn't right and he wasn't sure how to deal with it. His main concern was the strange look on the face of the child and the considerable length of time she'd been in the hut with the woman.

Finally, he got tired of watching and went home. And then the following day, he heard rumours that a little girl by the name of Sia Kpayagula had gone missing. As he heard the description of the missing girl, he quickly realised that the child he'd seen in the hut's window was the missing girl. There'd been an impending storm that night, just as there was tonight, Kaikai Lango remembered. He made his way to the window where he'd last seen the child. Peeping through the window he was able to make out the figure of a little girl lying silently on a raffia mat on the floor. She was alone in the hut. She'd been frightened by his soft knock on the window but she'd remained calm, staring blankly.

Quietly he knocked again. With a meekness that matched her feminine nature, Sia Kpayagula came gingerly toward the window until she could see Kaikai Lango smiling encouragingly at her. And then she recognized the man she'd seen earlier. As soon as an understanding was created he'd no issue at gaining Sia's confidence. He opened the unlocked window. The little girl's movements were sluggish and strangely clumsy. It wasn't until the window had been opened and he'd smelt an herbal odour in the hut that he became aware she might be on drugs. As he maneuvered Sia out the window, he held his breath against the stinging smell of a smoking incense. She creeped out wearing only the same white loincloth he'd seen her in earlier. Accepting his hushed tips, she remained really silent as they made their way across the farm through the storm to the community chief's house. Discreetly, he abandoned her on the verandah.

Throughout the walk Sia Kpayagula told him how her adopted mother accused her of being a witch and hence handed her over to the other woman for exorcism. At least the side effects of the smoking incense, Kaikai Lango had pondered, was that they appeared to have eased the hysterical agony the little girl would have experienced. Sia didn't seem to know exactly how much time had gone by since she'd been abducted.

Kaikai Lango had never discussed about Sia's disappearance from the hut with anybody although the other woman knew of his knowledge of it. Hence her last words to him some time ago. I want your assurance that you'll never disclose to anyone the story of the little child that you found in my farm hut.

So, as Kaikai Lango continued to walk with Jebbeh, she realised that they were heading towards Massa's room. He knocked on her door. And lo and behold, Massa dashed outside screaming for mercy. They heard the indication of restrained fright in her voice. He drew his breath. "It must be that evil," he inferred uncomfortably.

"Evil is a gentle word for the way I feel at any moment I think about those false allegations against me," Jebbeh told him very sincerely.

Like a person possessed by evil spirit, Massa ran directly to Jebbeh's doorstep, grabbed the clay pentacle, the black-handled double-edged dagger, and continued running into the dark forest. The air became cooler. Owls circled the trees. Insects thronged the night. Massa, the woman with the jewelled eyes, became the other woman who later confessed to the practice of witchcraft. As to how she went out to the witches' coven, Massa said she would spiritually put her household to sleep, turn into smoke and pass under the door of the room. Once outside, she would turn into a bat and fly away. Three days later Massa was found dead hanging from a palm tree.

NO FISH ON SUNDAYS

Elizabeth L. A. Kamara

"No! No! I can't do it. I can't…I don't even know why you think I will eat this. I cannot eat fish on Sundays!"

The nurses opened their mouths to the widest o and their eyes became saucers. They stood there as if frozen by medusa. The light skinned Nurse Kamara was holding a bowl of pepper soup and fish on the tray, and the dark-skinned Nurse Kamanda was about to drive the trolley close to the woman on the bed.

"Jolit, eat the food dear, you need the strength." Mr. Tokumbor-Coker patted his wife's back and removed an ant that was crawling on her shoulder.

She shook her head, looked at the maids, looked at the food, pursed her lips and sighed. They wanted her to *set yay bet fatfut,* but she will not do it. She could see the flowers on the small patio from her position on the bed. Every now and then, the fragrance of the flowers wafted into her bedroom. Her sense of smell has been playing the abiku on her ever since she contracted Covid 19. On the wall opposite, there was a calendar with the picture of a huge marlin that made her think of Hemingway's *The Old Man and the Sea*. It also brought her mind back to the food given to her. Her old anger that she had laid to rest when she saw the flowers, resurfaced.

"Fish on Sunday! Fish on Sunday! *If ah bin die yesterday, dis bin for pas me.* Fish on Sunday! Hmmm. Hm. Ah! Noooor." She shook her head and rolled her eyes in disappointment. Even though she was sick, everyone could tell that she was a beautiful woman. Her hair was plaited very neatly in a style known as *pot korba* and she had small lips, a small pointed nose and large piercing eyes. Everyone at the EldJohn Baptist Hospital knew her because she was the only female patient in that hospital who applied her makeup every day. Some of the nurses used to look at her and laugh behind her back at how she was so particular about her looks, even on a sick bed. For his part, her husband was happy that she was taking an interest in life by putting on cosmetics and reading.

" *Di mami,* the soup is very nice ma. We used snapper, but removed the bones. It does not even have a lot of pepper. Try it and see ma," Nurse Kamanda volunteered. " Di mami! Don't call me Di mami. Don't you ever call me Di mami again! Slack! You people are too slack! Di mami! I am Mrs. Tokumbor- Coker. Call me by my name, not Di mami!"

The nurse was apologetic.

"Sorry ma, I am so sorry. It will not happen again."

Jolit waved her hand and a semi smile flitted across her face.

"That's alright."

"Yes ma," ventured the nurse who bought her light skin, from the shops or hawkers, *"the peppeh soup sweet o, na the chief cook sef-sef kuk am"*. Nurse Kamara smiled and put the bowl of soup on the trolley. Her friend brought the trolley close to Jolit.

Jolit looked at the food with unsmiling eyes and pursed lips. She crossed her hands over her chest and looked away from the food, away from her husband and away from the nurses.

She missed the comfort of her home. She missed her home food. She missed her dog Sazzy and knew that Sazzy will be searching all over the house for her and wondered whether her houseboy, Orteim, will be feeding the dog thrice a day. She remembered that by that time of the year, the lilies would be out. Oh what a joy it would have been to see them lining the curb and peeping playfully amongst the stones. She missed her garden, especially the roses, sunflowers and pansies close to her bedroom window. Her house was perched on top of Sierra Hill, less than a minute's walk away from the famed Fourah Bay College (FBC)

Her eyes strayed to the bowl of pepper soup and instant revulsion gripped her. She had nothing against the pepper soup. She loved it. She would have eaten it with joy had they not prepared it with fish. Fish! The very thought made her shudder. Fish! Fish on Sunday!

She wanted to go back to her structured home. But here she had been hospitalized for five days so far and the doctor had not yet told her when she would go home. She no longer experienced fever, had stopped throwing up and her appetite had gradually returned.

These people wanted her to eat fish on a Sunday, just because she was hospitalized. She will not do it. In her home, she followed a rigorous menu pertaining to the different days of the week. Anyone in her household could travel for years and return home on any day of the week and still know what will be served because food was prepared according to the days of the week.

Mondays were days for eating the left over *Satiday plasas*. And Saturday sauces were **draw soup** (*kren-kren* or okra) and aegusi soup (***bitas/ sawa-sawa/shakpa***) on alternate Saturdays. Meat stew (any meat – chicken, lamb, cow meat, and pig's trotters) was cooked on Sundays. You do not eat fish on Sundays. You do not even put a little fish in the meat stew…it was just not done. Fish stew was prepared on Tuesdays and Fridays. Fish stew means just that – strictly fish, no meat. Tuesdays were actually just for fish stew, though on Fridays, fish stew could be interchanged with palm oil stew or black-eyed beans. Wednesdays and Thursdays were days on which groundnut soup or potato leaves or cassava leaves sauce was prepared.

She had never eaten fish on a Sunday, in all her 67 years on earth. Had it not been for sickness that brought her two feet to the hospital, she would never have found herself in a place where they offered fish on Sundays. She did not want to eat it! How will it even slide down her throat? Had she died yesterday or even 30 minutes ago, this cup, would have passed her. Her beloved parents and grandparents will be turning in their graves to know that she, Jumoke Omodele Latile Iyabo Tokumbor-Coker is being offered fish on a Sunday.

"Please darling, eat the food. You know that this is a private hospital and they do not allow people to bring in their own cooked meals."

She heard the voice of her husband, imploring her to eat. She turned her head and saw her husband pleading with his eyes. He stroked her hair and marvelled at his wife's beauty; nothing can detract from her beauty, nothing - sickness, anger, frustration –nothing. "Jolit," he urged gently, "Jolit, eat your food. You need to eat. You need to regain your energy. You can't get well if you don't eat. Do it for me. Do it for us."
She pouted.

"*Una go normor*," he waved to both the coffee colored and fair-skinned nurses.
"She will eat the food".

As the nurses were about to step out, he called them and gave them Nle 20 each. Their faces lit up as soon as they saw the money. They thanked him and smiled very broadly swinging their hands as they left.

Mr. Tokumbor-Coker turned to Jolit. "Come on Jolit, please eat the food. Fish is very good for your health you know. And it is not as if you do not eat fish at all."

" I know. But you know that Sunday is not fish stew day. It is not done. How can they expect me to eat fish on God's Sunday?" She pouted and shut her eyes as if that will take the pepper soup away from the room.

Her husband placed her hands gently round the pepper soup bowl. She drew them away as if she was scorched by the poker used by Absalom to brand Nicholas's bottom, or as if someone had stepped on her *kaktoe*.

"Jolit, please eat your food".

A note of firmness had crept into his voice. It rolled off his lips and hung in the air above them. Jolit had caught it. She knew that her husband was so close to losing his patience. He placed her hands around the bowl again and urged her to eat. She did not remove her hands from the bowl again, but made no attempt to eat. She looked into the bowl for the first time, and saw the fish in the pepper soup. There were four big chunks of fish, several chunks of Irish and sweet potato and the soup itself. The aroma of the soup tantalized her nostrils and she involuntarily swallowed some saliva. She did not know what to do. Her husband scooped a spoon of the pepper soup, without the fish and gave it to her. She parted her lips slowly, as if they were frozen and were being thawed on their own.

"Eat for my sake, if you don't want to eat for yourself. Eat for your children so that you can come back home quickly to us," Mr. Tokumbor-Coker beamed at her.

She tasted the first spoon and was surprised that it was very yummy. He gave her the second spoon and she enjoyed that too. She suddenly realized that she was hungry. She was surprised that she was looking forward to having more of the soup. This time around, when her husband gave her the soup, he added a bit of the fish to it. She was reluctant to taste the fish. But agreed to do so after he encouraged her to and tried to make her laugh. She opened her lips wide. She wanted to swallow the fish without allowing it to touch her tongue for a millisecond. She wanted to swallow the fish whole like the great fish swallowed Jonah whole, without chewing him at all. Hopefully, the fish in her mouth will not last three days in her stomach. She shut her eyes and attempted to swallow the fish. But then the fish touched her tongue and it tasted - like fish. It was delicious. She thought that since it was fish on a Sunday, it would taste strange. But it tasted like normal fish and she enjoyed it. She thought about her mother and grandmother, women who never cooked or ate fish on Sundays, and wondered whether they will literally turn in their graves. Her forebears were women who had never strayed from the menu and she had followed strictly in their footsteps. But after eating the fish on that Sunday, she decided that she will stick to the routine but will not hesitate to breach it if there is an emergency. She thought about the cost of living – the dollar that was soaring like a meteor, the price of fuel that was chasing the sky like a skylark, the prices of food and other basic commodities that were spiraling out of control like rebels – and thanked God that at least she and her husband can afford to maintain their daily menu. She was not sure about what will happen in the future. She was not sure, whether her three girls will follow in her footsteps regarding the daily menu, or even whether they will each have two **sol kop**, like her, her mother and grandmother.

Her husband wondered what was going through her mind, and was relieved and happy that she ate the fish without looking as if she was taking *gbangba*. He was thankful. He was certain that Godfather Death would not take his wife away so soon. Jolit will regain her health and they will go back home to fish stew on Tuesdays and Fridays and meat stew on Sundays.

Child Bride

Oumar Farouk Sesay

Eleven-year-old Ariatu wrenched her gaze from the road winding its way through the school to focus on Madam Bendu standing a few feet away from her. Ariatu's continuous musing about the road, pedestrians, and destination had gotten her into trouble several times with Madam Bendu. The road always put her mind into a light mood, and she mused where that road might take her in the day; she would summon the courage to run away from her predicament. Arguably for a girl promised to a husband when she was in the cradle, the road seemed to be the only way to freedom. Nevertheless, she could not afford to let her mind frolic into lonely places today, mainly when Madam Bendu needed her undivided attention in class.

Madam Bendu rang the bell to alert the pupils, who seemed tired after the lunch break.

"Class, we will do a career exercise this afternoon," she said. She then paused and pointed at the eleven-year-old Amara, who sat in the front row.

"What would you like to become in the future?" Amara stood up and scratched his head as if to put his thought in gear.

"I would like to be an Agriculturist to grow enough food to feed all the hungry people in the country, "said Amara confidently.

"You mean you want to be a farmer?" queried John mockingly. "You can be a farmer right now; you don't have to wait for the future," he concluded, sparking giggling and laughter among the class six pupils.

But Ariatu did not laugh because the career exercises put her in a soul-sapping mood. She had constantly been told she was only going to be a housewife. She continuously questioned the injustice of taking the freedom of choice from girls while boys were left to be what they wanted to become. She had often seen girls barely older than her being married off; and had always continually wished she could stop these spectacles of child-brides.

"Be quiet, everyone; you think farming is a joke? On the contrary, we would not be alive without farmers," cautioned Madam Bendu.

"So, what about you, John, what would you like to be when you grow up?" asked teacher Bendu.

John stood up and walked majestically to the front of the class; "Fellow pupils, I would like to be the Minister of Agriculture, so I will tell Amara what to plant".

"No, John, you won't be a minister just yet; be something first before you go into politics," said Madam Bendu. The class roared with laughter, and chants of the Minister of Agriculture were everywhere.

The tall and lean Salifu stood up and spoke confidently, like someone who knew what he wanted to become before he even came to school.

"I want to be a writer to write my country's stories."

Aziz was next to speak, "I want to be a lawyer to defend the poor people."

"I would like to be a doctor to cure the sick people in the village," said Hassan.

The chant of 'Doctor Hassan, Doctor Hassan' was everywhere. And one student remarked, "Doctor, my head is hurting." Another reported his tooth before Madam Bendu interrupted.

"It seems we have a class of would-be professionals, but I haven't heard a word from the girls," teased Teacher Bendu.

"Go on, Jatu, say something," said John. The other boys joined in urging her," Jatu! Jatu!" chanted the boys as they beat the desks in excitement.

Jatu stood up slowly and spoke in a low voice, "I want to be a midwife to help women deliver safely."

There was silence after she spoke before the boisterous John broke the silence, "Jatu, you want to be a midwife when you can be a doctor? You gave all of us a hard time in the sciences! What is happening to you?"

Before Jatu could respond, Ariatu stood up from the middle row and spoke in a much more audible voice than Jatu," I want to become someone who stops wrong things from happening to young girls."

"Ariatu, you are among the top-performing pupils in class; you can be anything you want to be," said Amara.

"Why would you want to be something more when your dad gave your hand in marriage to a man from the day you were born. You have to stop that first before you become someone else," countered Ariatu.

A deafening silence boomed across the classroom, sucking the joyous afternoon mood at the school.

Madam Bendu paced the classroom. She paused by Ariatu's desk. Ariatu looked at her, in a way that was both fatalistic and aspirational, and said, "all the women I know are housewives and, at best, midwives and few teachers; I have never seen a woman lawyer or Engineer."

"I had seen a woman judge when I went on holiday to the city, "said John.

Madam Bendu thought for a while and said, "I have an idea. Next week, we are going on a field trip to see male and female lawyers, judges, and doctors at their workplaces. Then, we shall repeat this career exercise when we return from the field trip."

The class burst into celebration, beating the desks and chanting.

The following week they boarded a bus to the city. As they got closer to the city, Madam Bendu gave the pupils pep talks on what to do and what not to do during the expedition. She told them to comport themselves as if they were in the classroom. Ariatu listened attentively as teacher Bendu explained that the trip was being sponsored and coordinated by an organization called Purposeful with a mission to expand opportunities for the girl child to be more than just homemakers.

"Our first stop will be the law court, where judge Rugia is presiding. Girls, it would help if you cover your heads with a head tie to show respect for the courtroom. It would be best if you all comported yourself as you do in the classroom. Are you listening to me?"

"Yes, Madam Bendu," shouted the pupils.

Ariatu marveled at the tall buildings, the traffic, and the neatly dressed people going to their offices.

The bus arrived at the courthouse. The pupils disembarked and walked in a single file to the courtroom, presided over by Judge Rugia. As soon as they entered the courtroom, Judge Rugia welcomed them. "We welcome the class six pupils of Alhusine Memorial of Masingbi. We are glad to have you in our courtroom. Take the second-row seats reserved for you".

"Thank you, madam Judge," replied the pupils.

"Silence in court, Honourable Rugia Sesay presiding," the court clerk announced.

"Counsel for the defense, proceed," ordered the Judge.

"My lord, my client cannot be charged with a sexual offense because he is legally married to the witness," argued the defense lawyer.

"Objection, my Lord, the witness, this young survivor, cannot be said to be legally married to accused because she is sixteen years old. Therefore, she is below the age of consent as captured in the 2017 Sexual Offenses Act," argued the prosecution lawyer.

"Objection sustained," the Judge affirmed banging her gavel on the table.

Ariatu admired the Judge and the court system. As soon as the Judge adjourned the case, she walked straight to the Judge. "Madam Judge, I want to be just like you when I grow up".

"Young woman, you can be more than a judge if you work hard," the Judge replied.

"I am ready to work hard to be like you, Madam," said Ariatu

"I will see that you get the guidance you need; thank you for coming".

"You welcome, madam Judge," remarked the pupils.

The expedition left the courthouse for the hospital to see the inner workings of the biggest health center in the nation. But Ariatu's mind seemed to have stuck on the lawyer's objection about the age of consent in marriage.

"Good afternoon, pupils," said the graceful, but authoritative Dr. Rashida.

"Good afternoon, doctor," responded the pupils.

"I am Doctor Rashida, given the responsibility by the hospital management to show you what we do in this hospital."

"Thank you very much, doctor, for your time," said Madam Bendu.

"Doctor Rashida, what is that thing around your neck?" asked Jatu.

"This is a stethoscope; we use it to check the patient's vital signs like, heartbeats and lung function," replied Dr. Rashida.

"How about this place?" Jatu asked again.

"This is the outpatient ward; where we attend to patients who stay in their homes but come here regularly about for treatment. Please follow me so I can show you the entire hospital operations," replied Rashida.

"What unit is that with so many frail-looking girls?" asked Ariatu.

"That is the fistula unit. It deals with young girls mostly given to husbands before they are sexually mature; and women with birth-related complications, " replied Dr. Rashida.

The pupils asked many questions and learned much about radiography and tropical diseases before they ended the conducted tour.

At the end of the tour, the pupils boarded the bus. They returned to the village, chanting, and teasing each other's chosen professions. The objection in the courtroom on the age of sexual consent and the talk about fistula wedged two daggers in Ariatu's heart as she took her window seat at the back of the bus.

The bus arrived at the school compound, and the students disembarked and were dispatched to their various homes for the weekend filled with hopes and dreams they had never dreamt before.

Ariatu excitedly explained to her Mum about the trip, the fun, and the woman judge who promised to mentor her.

"Mum, you should see the Judge in her gown and wig judging cases. The verdict; I want to be a judge," affirmed Aritau.

Ariatu's eyes met her Mum's eyes; she froze as she saw tears dripping from her Mum's eyes.

"What happened, Mum? Why are you crying? Did someone die while we were away?"

"Ariatu, my beloved, no one died. It is your dad…"

Before she could complete her statement, Ariatu cut in, "Is my dad okay, mummy?"

Yabu held her daughter closely as if she wanted to return her to the womb via her chest. She preferred her daughter lodged safely within the sanctity of her womb than to tell her what she was about to say to her.

"When you left for your trip, the man your dad betrothed you to was here to see your dad and asked for your hand in marriage."

"But Mum, I am a child. I am only an eleven-years-old, Mum. I want to be a judge, not a wife, at least not now and not to a man of my father's age."

"I agree with you entirely, my daughter. You have a right to pursue your dreams and not be forced to marry like we were forced to marry immediately after our initiation ceremony."

"Mum, where is dad? I need to talk to him about the age of consent and fistula."

"Your dad went out; he might return late. But, meanwhile, go have your dinner and shower till we think of a way out of this dilemma."

Ariatu disengaged from the hug and retreated to her room sobbing. That night she couldn't eat or shower. Her mind was laden with a burden she couldn't carry. She woke up from her disturbed sleep to do her morning chores, hoping to talk to Pa Kargbo, her father, about the marriage issue. She had rehearsed throughout the night about what to tell him and how to say it to avoid pricking her dad's anger and stubbornness. She planned to tell him about her dreams of becoming a judge like the judge she saw on the school expedition to the city. She hoped to remind him about the meeting the NGO, Purposeful held at the town hall some time ago to educate parents about underage marriages and the need to give the girl child equal opportunities to enable them to attain their dreams. She planned to tell him about the girls with fistula. She was lost in her thought when her dad entered the pantry where she was ironing her uniform. Before she could greet him, her dad spoke first.

"Where do you think you are going with that uniform? Haven't you spoken to your mother? There is no more schooling for you".

"But, dad, I don't want to get married; I am too young to be married. Instead, I have my dreams of becoming a judge. So, it is unjust to do this to me," replied Ariatu.

"You talking back to me? You speak back when I speak to you? Talking back to me is exactly why this school thing must end now to halt this aggressive conduct," snarled Pa Kargbo. "In fact, give me the uniform. School ends today. After you are married, if your husband decides to send you to school to become a judge over him, it is his business. I will not allow you to be in my house and get pregnant like our neighbour's daughter. Not on my watch," continued Pa Kargbo as he pulled the uniform from Ariatu's grip.

Ariatu ran in distress to the end of town towards the Chief's compound, searching for a solution to her dilemma. The eldest wife of the Chief, Nakama, saw Ariatu as she arrived in distress at the palace.

"What happened, my daughter?" queried Nakama. Ariatu tried to speak, but the crying and sobbing took away the audibility of her voice.

"Calm down, Ariatu; take a deep breath and calm down; it is not the world's end. Whatever it is, we will findnd a solution," said Nakama.

"It is the end of the world that I know and want. My dad took my uniform and said I shouldn't go to school again till I get married," cried Ariatu.

Nakama held Ariatu close to her chest, consoling her as her

mother reassured her when she was in distress. Then, Nakama cleared her throat and stared straight into Ariatu's eyes before she spoke to her.

"Young girl, listen to me keenly; your dad is renowned for his strong- headedness, so you need to go home and sit calmly till the chief return from attending the Purposeful work at Magburaka. I will put your case to him when he returns".

"I heard you, Ma, thank you very much, Ma," replied Ariatu with a fragile voice projecting the brokenness inside her. Ariatu left the palace for nowhere in particular. But her muscle memory took her to the school, and to her classroom just as the career exercise was about to begin.

"Court rise, Honourable Justice Ariatu Kargbo in attendance," announced John in jest. The entire classroom reeled with laughter; even Madam Bendu enjoyed the joke. But Ariatu's soul-shattering cry rang across the room, shredding the laughter into shards.

Madam Bendu, a teacher of so many decades, knew the timbre of that cry because she had heard it before from girls pulled from school and given to husbands against their wish. That kind of cry came from a place of despair and vulnerability. Madam Bendu sidled through the desk to hug and console Ariatu. She did not need to ask what happened. She knew the cry that sounded like a funeral song for the death of a girl's education. She held her close to her chest and whispered to her ears, "My dear, it will be okay, don't worry, my darling, you will be a judge someday".

Pa Kargbo burst into the classroom in commando style and grabbed Ariatu from the bosom of Bendu like a hawk catching a chick.

Madam Bendu held on to one arm, refusing to let go; the pupils joined the tug of war, pulling Ariatu in a different direction. Jatu withdrew from the brawl to capture the scene with her phone.

"Pa Kargbo, don't do this to your daughter; she is too young to be married. She is only eleven years old," snapped Bendu.

"What I do with my daughter is none of your business or the government's or Purposeful's," snarled Pa Kargbo.

The uproar shattered the serenity of the school until the headmaster came to calm the situation. Eventually, Ariatu was taken from school like a lamb to the marital slaughterhouse. Jatu and other girls gathered in silos weeping for their friend and fate. They cried for those before and after them in case this status quo was to remain the same.

Pa Kargbo wasted no time in arranging the marriage for her daughter. He set a date for the wedding, and preparation began in earnest.

Ariatu was kept in seclusion as the preparation continued. She pined in her semi-prison to reach out to someone who could help end her nightmare. Finally, Yabu came to cajole Ariatu to eat; and she showed her the white lace and veil the would-be husband brought her to wear on the wedding day.

"My daughter, I am sorry, there is nothing I can do; your dad threatened to throw us from the house and disown you and your siblings".

"Mum, I prefer he disowns me than putting me through this form of death."

"My daughter, to be disowned by your father is like being cast away, like heaping a curse on you. I don't want that for you and your siblings."

"My dad is already casting me away by giving my hand in marriage at this age and killing my dream," retorted Ariatu as she threw the white wedding dress on the floor.

Yabu picked up the dress and tried to console her daughter.

"Mum, that dress and veil look to me like a shroud; Mum do something, or I will rather die than do this," she sobbed and leaned on her Mum. They both cried.

"My daughter, I wish I could remove us from this trap. However, I am still hopeful that Nakama will convey your plight to the Chief before this marriage happens on Thursday".

"Mum, our days should not be like your days; there must be something we can do. Where is my phone?"

"Sadly, your dad dumped it in the pit latrine," replied Yabu. Ariatu shook her head despondently.

"How about my friend Jatu? Can I see her in my jail?" retorted Ariatu sarcastically.

"She came to see you several times, but your dad refused her access, but I told her to come again when your dad leaves for the maghrib prayers".

After Yabu left, Ariatu continued to ponder the way out of the trap and the way forward. She knew her solution lay in reaching out to those in authority. She recalled the visit of Purposeful NGO and their message about creating a safe space for the girl child, and about stopping early marriages for the girl child. She remembered the director speaking about bringing change to a male-dominated society. She recalled the director saying they must be proactive and stand up for themselves as girls. But, above all, she recalled the conclusion of his talk when he told them that Purposeful would give girls a shoulder to lean on in times of need. At that juncture, a light bulb lit up in Ariatu's mind, and the sense of knowing calmed her mind.

The azan for the Maghrib prayer rang through the air as her room/ cell door opened to usher in Jatu. Ariatu hugged Jatu, and they both cried.

"I will leave you together while I keep watch for the return of your dad from the Mosque; I don't want to get into additional trouble again," said Yabu. "Please keep it quiet here," she cautioned them before leaving the room.

The girls acknowledged Yabu's exit and continued their dialogue.

"Jatu, did you bring your phone?" Ariatu asked as if her life depended on the reply.

"Ariatu, I have more than just a phone; I have a clip of the incident at school," replied Jatu, as she showed the video clip to Ariatu.

"This clip is more than what I need, darling; you are a lifesaver," said Ariatu excitedly.

"I will do everything for you, my sister," replied Jatu.

"I know you will; that is why I want you to caption this video because the letters on your phone are so faded, I can't even spell my name on it," Ariatu teased

. They laughed with the joy of a prisoner who had just stolen the key to the jail from the sleeping jail keeper.

"If you are against the abuse of the girl child, and if you are against early marriages. Please forward this video of a girl of eleven years forcefully removed from school to be married to a sixty-year-old man. Forward this video till it got to PURPOSEFUL and other organizations to stop the abuse," dictated Ariatu.

"Done; do you want to read it before we post?" Asked Jatu. "You are the only person who can read from the crack screen of your phone, so you read what you have typed," giggled Ariatu. Jatu laughed as she read the words dictated to her. Then, Jatu highlighted five WhatsApp groups and asked Ariatu to press the forward button. She pressed the button, and the message left her home prison to get to the whole wide world. So, the news rode on the tide of human compassion until it came to the handset of the Purposeful director, who tried to set things right.

Meanwhile, Pa Kargbo went ahead with the arranged marriage, not knowing that the machinery of Purposeful was stomping toward him like a derailed freight train.

In the days leading to the wedding, older women tended to Ariatu. They washed her, exfoliated her skin, oiled her, and dressed her daily. The beauticians placed indigo dye from leaves on her palms and feet to make beautiful geometric patterns on her body. She looked like a blossoming flower but a flower soon to be deflowered and left to wither away.

The wedding dress of lace materials was like a white shroud to her. They sprayed her with expensive Arabia perfumes, but to her they smelled like the fragrance of the dead. They sang and danced in celebration, but to her, it sounded like a funeral, and the beauticians were like morticians to her. For Ariatu, marriage was the death of her dream of becoming a judge; it was the death of joy; it was social death. She pondered what she would have in common with a husband old enough to be her grandfather.

Ariatu felt like cattle when two older women came to her on her father's request to look at her. She couldn't understand what they meant until the women came and started to probe her like gynecologists. After examining her, they clapped with joy and pronounced it to everyone.

"We should prepare for *mayaraytate* dance; joyfully, we have a woman of chastity here," said the old woman. "Yabu, you are a wonderful mother to have delivered a virgin bride".

The other woman ululated to inform the household of many

wives that the bride was a virgin. Then the two older women left the room to convey the prize message to Pa Kargbo and Sheku, the groom. Ariatu pieced together the full import of the proof of her virginity. She deduced the purpose of what marriage was about to the groom. She retrieved the bits of information about motherhood and childbirth. She knew she would soon be made a baby with babies if she didn't run for her life. Ariatu saw the tearful yet cheerful face of her Mum. Ariatu saw a streak of joy in her Mum's eyes trailing after the tears and wondered why.

"Mum, I feel like a slave about to be sold without her consent, and I see joy and sorrow on your face. I can understand the sorrow but not the joy. How and where can you find joy when your daughter is in a dilemma".

"My daughter, one of the women who came to check you, told me that someone told Sheku that you are no longer a virgin, so Sheku demanded that he marries you now," replied Yabu.

"What were they expecting? I am only an eleven-year-old girl," cried Ariatu.

Jatu heard the ululation and the singing; she sneaked into the room, covering her face with a veil to avoid detection.

"Jatu, why are you dressed like an old woman?" asked Ariatu.

"I am afraid of your dad; I don't want him to detect me, of course," replied Jatu. "I need to update you; the sap we sent has gone viral, and Madam Bendu received a call from the Purposeful director. The director has informed the Chief".

Before Ariatu could respond, Jatu sneaked out again, "I thought I heard your dad's voice. I should go now but let me assure you that you will not be a slave".

"What is it about?" questioned Yabu.

"Do you want to know? I don't think so because I don't want your husband to blame you for my action," commented Ariatu.

"My daughter, I put my trust in you, and you didn't fail me; you have proven to me that you are not what they thought you were. As always, I am behind you. Anything that will take you from this trap, do it".

On the wedding day, Sheku, the groom, sent in his family members with money, dowry, and gifts to conduct the wedding. As traditions demanded, a small token of cash called bora was given to every community member, from the kids to the Paramount Chief and imams. The groom's family put the dowry in a calabash with other items like cola nuts, pin, thread, and mat. Each item in the calabash is a symbolic representation of the trials of marriage. The hook and thread are for the wife to stay true to the promise of better or worse and be willing to stitch her husband's clothes in days of hardship; the white cloth is sexual fidelity to the husband; and the kola about respect for the bride's famiy.

Ariatu could hear the proceedings in her room or, better still, jail.

Sheku's elder brother, Okama who led the delegation, spoke in a firm voice that belied his age. "We, the Kamara family of Mamuntha, greet you with good tidings. We are here this afternoon for a purpose, but before we proceed, we will love to have the family give us a person through whom we will pass our message".

Ariatu heard muffled whispers before the voice of her uncle Foday stood out among the many voices. "The elders of the Kargbo family have agreed to make me the *sababu* and guarantor of the marriage".

Okama acknowledged Foday as *sababu* by shaking his hand with a bora of four thousand leones. Foday accepted the bora and gave the floor to the delegation leader to Okama to continue. He took a bundle of envelopes containing the *boras* for the girls, boys, women, men, grandmothers, aunts, stepmothers, mothers, fathers, imams, and Chiefs. Okama gave the boras to the *sababu*, prefixing each *bora* with a speech of parables and nuanced language developed over the years for occasions like this.

"I will stop until the *boras* are accepted before moving to the next phase. I don't want the Kargbos to worry. There is abundant money here to give to them so long as they give us what we want," said Okama. His comment triggered giggles and laughter, giving the Yelimusu a cue to heap praise on the Kamara family.

She sang honouring the family's lineage, beginning from its origin. This brought showers of cash to her.

Foday made the shahadat - bearing testimony that there is a single God and Mohamed is His prophet- to silence the crowd. After getting their attention, he started distributing the *boras* to those they were meant for, or their representatives. Each acceptance of the bora sealed the fate of Ariatu. Then Foday got to the bora for the Chief, "do we have a representative of the Chief here to take his bora?" he asked.

The honking of a horn and the sound of a skidding vehicle on the graveled road reached Ariatu. She peeped at the window and saw the car of the Paramount Chief outside. There was a flurry of greetings and homage to the Chief before the place calmed down. Foday briefed the Chief and passed the envelope containing the *bora* to the Chief.

"Before I receive the bora, I need some answers to questions about the bride and bridegroom. You recalled a meeting at the town hall where I informed you that Parliament had passed a new law called the Sexual Offenses Act?" asked the Chief.

A chorus of affirmative responses filled the air. Ariatu and the chaperone peeped at the window for a clearer view of what was happening on the patio.

"Do you also recall that after the law was passed, an organization called Purposeful came here and held a workshop to educate us on the benefits of the girl child's education and the danger of early marriages?" asked the Chief.

The affirmative answer rang through the verandah like a response to prayer.

The Chief sipped from the water bottle he was holding, cleared his throat, and continued his address. "I am just coming from a workshop Purposeful organized for the paramount chiefs of the district, and they gave us a form to guide us in implementing the law. As a result, we as leaders have agreed and signed that we will not take a wedding *bora* without receiving satisfactory answers to the following questions".

From the window, Ariatu could see the crestfallen faces of Sheku and her dad. She could also see the giggle on Madam Bendu's face and the ripple of movement from people trying to sneak out.

"No one should move out of this gathering until we are done with this wedding," commanded the Chief. Then, the Chief called on Madam Bendu from the crowd to help fill the form.

Madam Bendu moved through the crowd to occupy a chair close to the Chief, who handed her two forms to fill.

"Beginning now, this form must be filled before any marriage in this chiefdom is approved. As it is a norm to give a *bora* to the Chief, it will also be mandatory to fill this form before a marital *bora* is accepted, "proclaimed the Chief.

Then, the Chief called for both bride and groom to come forward as he ordered Madam Bendu to fill the form, starting with the names of both bride and groom, the address, occupation, marital status, and age.

After a prolonged debate and cumulating of historical evidence, it became clear that the groom, Sheku was sixty-five years old and the bride eleven years.

"This is a case of a man marrying a child fit to be his granddaughter and a father selling his daughter for money," fumed the Chief.

"Chief, I am not selling my daughter; I am marrying her off like our mothers were married at prime age," replied the angry Kargbo.

"That was then, and this is now. And the law now states that any marriage in which the bride is below eighteen years is a crime. So, you and your grandfatherly brother-in-law are on the verge of committing a crime that carries a fifteen-year jail sentence". Ariatu sensed the shame shrinking his once towering father as he bowed his head.

The whispers and giggling stopped at the talk of crime and prison time. The Chief kept silent a shade longer as if to compose himself before he spoke in a measured tone and calibrated tenor.

"I would not be here to stop you from committing a crime had it not been for the viral video of you fighting with teachers and pupils to remove your daughter from school. If you only know where that video has gone, you would brace up

Ariatu stared in the direction of Jatu; their eyes met, and they both blinked in appreciation of their strategy.

The Chief shuffled the remaining bora envelopes, pulled out the one bearing his name, and turned to Foday, the guarantor of the wedding. "I am returning this *bora* through you to the groom. According to the new law of the land, this marriage is a crime, and as a ruler of this land, I won't be a party to it".

The boys and girls were next in line to return the *bora*, followed by all those given the *boras*, thus effectively dismantling the wedding.

Tears flowed from Ariatu's eyes as the Chief's pronouncement effectively cancelled her premature enslavement to a man she didn't love. She sobbed out loud as she kept repeating her dream of wanting to become a judge. Madam Bendu came forward to console her and wipe her tears with the veil.

The Chief stood up to respond to Ariatu's cry in a tone that gave hope to Ariatu and a subtle threat to Kargbo. "Ariatu, don't worry, you will become whatever you want to be and I believe I say so with the consent of your dad". He turned to Kargbo as he spoke.

Kargbo nodded his head in approval.

"I am thrilled to have had your dad's approval for you to continue your schooling. Therefore, I am delighted to inform you that Purposeful organization has agreed to pay a visit to your school to meet all the pupils who stood up for education".

The Chief hugged Ariatu and consoled her before he left.

The groom's family grabbed their calabash and *boras* and sneaked out ingloriously.

Ariatu's classmate shouted, "objection my Lord'.

And Ariatu joyfully responded, "sustained."

The Golden Crown of Ordu

Art Koroma.

Today, in the very heart of Gbonkor-loko forest, there stands a very old cotton tree. It is older than any other tree and has seen many wonderful things. It is very wise too, and knows many secrets about the chiefdom's chieftaincy, culture, custom and tradition.

Every rainy season it sprouts into fresh green leaves and lovely white blossoms. But one year the flowers are more beautiful than ever; and, among them, on one of the lower branches, a bud hangs there like a silver globe among the green leaves.

"I wonder why that bud is so much larger and more beautiful than the others," says the breadfruit tree, who happens to be known for his curiosity.

"It holds a secret," replies the cola-nut tree, who is quite a gossip and loves to talk to the other trees.

"But when shall we know the secret?" asks the breadfruit tree.

"In the middle of the night there will be a thunder-storm and then the bud will open. You will see it by the lightning."

But when the storm comes, the thunder roars and the lightning flashes, the breadfruit tree is afraid and dreads to look up. But the cola-nut tree watches the grand old cotton tree stretch its branches out bravely to the tempest, and amidst it, he sees the white bud burst open as the third bough lays its blooms gently on the ground.

Inside the flower lay the prettiest little baby ever seen; there he curls up as if asleep, as lovely as a flower himself, and with his eyes wide opened. He lies smiling at the sky and watching the blue-white flashing across the clouds.

Then when morning comes and all around is bright, calm and still once more, the baby puts out his tiny hand and plays with the flowers.

"He must be a wonderful baby," says the cola-nut tree. "See his little white silk shirt; it is just the colour of the flower in which he is born; and what a wander to see that he has a shiny diamond on his forehead!"

"Perhaps it is a star and not a diamond," says the breadfruit tree; "but because of its brightness it can't known whether it's a star or diamond."

The cotton tree is one of the most sacred trees of our time. Our people consider it a deity or a home of many good children. Women who do not get pregnant so quickly will go in the shade of this tree to offer prayers and sacrifices.

On this day, the hummingbirds and the parrots and the monkeys and the jackals all stare up at the baby. "He would be better off if he had wings like mine," says a hummingbird.

"Or if he had plumage like mine," says a parrot.

"Fur like mine would be much better for him," adds a jackal.

But they all agree that he is a very wonderful baby, or he will not have a star on his forehead.

By and by the child cries just a little bit, for he is hungry, but the cola-nut tree bends its bough and drops a piece of cola-nut on his chest, and then he smiles again.

And then when sunset comes, a tigress steals quietly up to the child.

"I'll bring my cubs here," she says to herself. "He will do for their supper." But the flowers and the grasses cover him up so that she cannot find and gobble him up.

"We will not let any harm come to him," says the flowers and the grasses. "He is our baby."

"What shall we call him?" ask the trees.

And the older tree mother of the beautiful bud says, "His name is Orduray, in short, Ordu, meaning, the first human creature of the forest and all of you must take care of him and teach him the secrets of Gbonkor-loko forest."

And so, as Ordu grows up, the trees and the wildflowers and all the creatures in the forest teach him all they know. The monkeys teach him how to climb trees; and Dame, the great turtle, who lives in the river of Ro-loko, teaches him how to swim.

The hummingbirds show him where the wild fruits grow and which of the blossoms have nectar in their cups to make honey; and he learns the healing properties of the herbs; know which one will heal bruises, and how to charm the forest snakes, and many other things, which children who live in houses, hardly know. Early morning, he baths in the river of Ro-loko, hanging his white silk shirt to dry on a tree, and at night he sleeps in a hammock under the cola-nut tree, which the flowers weave with their twining tendrils for him.

As time goes on, he becomes a stout and beautiful boy, as good and gentle as he is strong and fearless. As for clothes, his white silk shirt grows without wear and tear. All the animals in the forest love him. Even the tigress who once wants her cubs to eat him as a baby has now affectionately warmed up to him.

One day Ordu says to the older tree, "There are great many parrots and jackals and monkeys. Are there no others like me; is there only one Ordu?"

And the older tree asks, "Why do you want to know?"

And Ordu replies wistfully, "I should like to see them."

Then the older tree says, "climb to my topmost branch, and tell me what you see."

And when Ordu has done this, he cries out, "I see a hill with a very sharp point."

"Near the top of that hill, which is the needle-shaped hill, is a tree covered with bright pink blossoms. It is called N'gberay," says the older tree. "Go up to it and smell the flowers and ask where the four brothers are."

So, through the forest Ordu runs to the needle-shaped hill, and there he finds N'gberay, the pink-flowering tree. "Where are the four brothers?" he asks, as he smells the blossoms.

"On the other side of the hill," says N'gberay. "They are preparing their supper."

Then Ordu goes on, around the hill, and there, he finds four tall men cutting up a deer, which they have just killed. As he draws near, they gaze at him and agree that they have never seen such a handsome boy and run to meet him. He is indeed a handsome boy, dressed all in white, the star shining on his forehead and a look of gentle love on his face.

"We are four brothers; will you be the fifth?" they ask Ordu. "Will you be one of us?"

"I will be your brother," replies Ordu, "for that is why I came. All the creatures in the forest have brothers and sisters, and I have none. I want to find some brethren."

Then Chernor, the youngest brother, says, "There is one thing we want - the fire to cook our meat. Unless we have fire, we are obliged to eat the flesh of the deer raw since there is no fire around."

Another brother Shekuna, the eldest says that the giant Paramount Chief Alikali has a fire burning in his hearth and three daughters who are anxious to get married. They know that he lives not very far away, but they have never been able to find his house, so they are still without fire to light the wood with which to cook the deer they have killed.

"If you will give me a bulrush," says Ordu, "I will show you the way to his house."

So Chernor brings him a bulrush and Ordu fits it to his bowstring; then he bends the bow, letting the bulrush fly straight to Paramount Chief Alikali's palace. "Follow my arrow," cries Ordu. "It has cleared a path for you, and you shall find what you want."

Then the four brothers follow the path Ordu's arrow has paved. Chernor, who is the swiftest runner, reaches the giant's palace first.

Paramount Chief Alikali is sleeping by the fire in a large room where the couches are twenty feet long and eight feet high. The fireplace is like a huge, red, glowing cavern in which whole tree-trunks lay burning instead of logs, and the ceiling is so high that Chernor can hardly see it.

Chernor glances at the sleeping giant and then snatches up a firebrand and runs for the door. But as he passes the sleeping giant, a spark from the brand falls on Paramount Chief Alikali's hand.

The giant springs up with a cry of pain and rushes out of the palace after Chernor but can hardly catch him. In his flight Chernor drops the firebrand and gets back to his brothers with nothing to show for his trouble but fright.

"We have to leave Paramount Chief Alikali alone," he tells them. "I would rather eat raw flesh all my life than go near that monster again."

Meanwhile, when the giant could not catch Chernor, he goes back to his palace and into the room where his wife and three daughters are. He is very cross, for he has lost his nap and a burn on his hand pains him.

As soon as he has thrown himself into his great chair, his oldest daughter asks him, "Have you got husbands for us now?"

Every day one of his daughters asks him this question and the sulky old giant will reply, "No! who can get husbands for three daughters all at once?"

Then the youngest daughter asks her father. "Papa, who was that young man that I saw running away from the palace?"

"While I was sleeping, a young man had come in and stolen a firebrand," their father replies.

"I think you did very wrong to send him away," says the giant's wife. "That would have been a way to get a husband for one of your daughters. For Paramount Chiefs' daughters do not get husbands easily. Here is the arrow that struck into the room this morning. This is a sign that men will soon follow it. You have done a very foolish thing and we shall probably suffer for it."

The Paramount Chiefs' wives are afraid of their husbands, but this one is not, and she goes on to give her husband such a scolding that Paramount Chief Alikali is glad to get away and go to sleep by the fire again.

After a while the Paramount Chief is awakened by a beautiful music, which comes from a tree that grows close to his palace wall. He lies still enjoying the sweet sounds, but presently they seem to draw him outside, and looking up he sees Ordu sitting on one of the branches of the tree playing on a 'kondi' an instrument like a lute.

Under the tree, the dogs, cats and all the other animals belonging to him are listening to the music. The birds are perched on the boughs underneath, listening too. Presently the music grows so merry that Paramount Chief Alikali holds up his agbada and begins to dance.

"What a silly old man you are!" cries his wife as she comes out of the palace and sees what he is doing. "You silly old man!" But in a few minutes, she is dancing too, holding up her lapa with one hand like a young girl, while her bangles and anklets tinkle merrily.

Then the Paramount Chief calls to Ordu, "Here, young man, come down from the tree and I will give you anything you want."

"Then you must give me your three daughters," says Ordu. "And you must give me, besides, a firebrand from your hearth."

"I knew the arrow was a true omen," cries the Paramount Chief's wife, and then his three daughters come forward and give Ordu his arrow, which they have carefully kept.

They are so pleased that they say good-bye to their father and mother; and in a hurry, they set about packing their clothes and jewels as they carry them on their heads in great haste to set out with Ordu.

They walk until they come to the needle-shaped hill toped with the pink-flowering N'gberay tree, where they marry Ordu and live very happily together.

The Paramount Chief Alikali later dies of old age. Ordu is happy to marry the three daughters of Paramount Chief Alikali; and, because he is better and wiser than they, the four brothers offer seven cola-nuts, seven cowries and white substance of rice powder to the gods of Gbonkor-loko. Introducing Ordu as their future Paramount Chief.

The next day, the sunlight beams through the clear blue sky and into the tropical trees in the midst of a blistering afternoon.

The Lokomasama high priest, known as Pa-Shinneh Korthai, dances his way from middle of the sacred river of Ro-loko towards the sacred cotton tree of Gbonkor-loko. He is now only a few meters away.

As he positions himself parallel to the center of the sacred cotton tree, he begins to stamp his feet. He licks his left-hand sun finger and places it in the air to help determine the direction of the wind. "When you change Paramount Chiefs, you change customs," ays Pa-Shinneh Korthai, who then signals for Ya-Bomkaprr, the ceremonial drummer, to follow his lead. Ya-Bomkaprr begins to match the pace of the high priest's feet with her drum, called thabulay. Pa-Shinneh Korthai then begins to lower his head and whirl his arms in a circular motion.

There is a sudden change of pace as he walks. He is now shuffling at an alarming speed. As he raises his head to look up at the sky, he speaks, "The Paramount Chief has now rightfully taken his place as the Paramount Chief of the Chiefdom. The elders have decided it is he who must lead us. Now we kindly ask that you seal this ceremony with the presence of the Golden Stool."

Pa-Shinneh Korthai's voice is now loud and clear. The announcement is heard throughout the entire ceremonial ground. The rhythm of the thabulay-drum continues as Pa-Shinneh Korthai begins to chant and dance. His voice grows louder and louder. A small magical fan commonly known as N'leffa suddenly appears in his right hand.

The high priest is now in a trance. As he dances, he waves the mystical fan in the four directions of the chiefdom. He starts off on his right side, then switches it over to his left, then behind him and finally in front of him. As he completes this motion, a chair-like figure appears above the cotton tree. It's a rare artifact known as the Golden Crown. You can hear the gasps and shocks from the villagers in the crowd. The royal crown slowly begins to descend as if Pa-Shinneh Korthai has slowed down time. He then calls over to Ordu, "Come young Paramount Chief. You must touch the Golden Crown."

Ordu proceeds towards the sacred cotton tree.

As he walks over, the high priest smiles, "Our ancestors and gods have accepted you as our Paramount Chief. To become a Paramount Chief and wear a crown is a thing more glorious to them that see it; just as it is pleasant to them that bear it. You have a mighty head and a big heart to fill into it, as you are born from a great thundering storm, which blows a strong wind into the bud of this great cotton tree in our sacred forest of Gbonkor-loko. But I have no doubt you will make us proud."

www.ingramcontent.com/pod-product-compliance
Lightning Source LLC
Chambersburg PA
CBHW031534210526
45464CB00013B/815